PAUL HARVEY'S THE REST OF THE STORY

Books by Paul Harvey

REMEMBER THESE THINGS

AUTUMN OF LIBERTY

THE REST OF THE STORY (1956)

YOU SAID IT, PAUL HARVEY

Paul Harvey's
The Rest of the Story

PAUL AURANDT

Edited and compiled by Lynne Harvey

DOUBLEDAY & COMPANY, INC., GARDEN CITY, NEW YORK

ISBN 0-385-12768-5
Library of Congress Catalog Card Number 77-75381
Copyright © 1977 by Paulynne, Inc.
All rights reserved
Printed in the United States of America

If you can look into the seeds of time,
And say which grain will grow and which will not,
Speak then to me. . . .

Shakespeare, *Macbeth* I, iii, 58–60

I wonder that a soothsayer doesn't laugh
whenever he sees another soothsayer.

Cicero, *De divinatione* II, xxiv

PROLOGUE

. . . and then there were three.
But first . . . THE REST OF THE STORY.

CONTENTS

12

14

PAUL HARVEY'S THE REST OF THE STORY

1. DR. PEMBERTON'S PICK-ME-UP

In the first place, Dr. Pemberton wasn't even a doctor. But who'd trust a product called "Mr. Pemberton's Triplex Liver Pills"?

No one.

Therefore he called it "Dr. Pemberton's Globe of Flower Cough Syrup" and "Dr. Pemberton's Extract of Styllinger Blood Medicine."

But if Dr. Pemberton wasn't a doctor, he also wasn't a quack. He merely lived in an era, right after the Civil War, when the corner druggist knew as much about medicines as the national drug manufacturers. And that's just what John Pemberton was. A corner druggist.

It was sometime after moving his business from Columbus to Atlanta—some while after "Dr. Pemberton's Indian Queen Hair Dye"—that this obscure Georgia pharmacist started fiddling with a basement brew you'll want to know about.

Most patent medicines in those days contained alcohol. None of that in John Pemberton's new concoction. In fact, according to some, he was trying to effect a headache cure . . . or perhaps a hangover cure for the other patent medicines.

John experimented with the extracts of fruits and nuts and leaves, but that was for taste. If he was going to cure a headache he'd need, perhaps, a stimulant? Yes. Caffeine. And an analgesic. Some say . . . cocaine.

Now it was all over but the selling. But John, who had spent most of his time developing this new pick-me-up, would need financial help. So, during the summer of 1886, Dr. Pemberton took a jug of the reddish-brown syrup to Jacobs Pharmacy, one of the most reputable in Atlanta.

What was in it, the manager wanted to know?

Dr. Pemberton explained that it was a secret but the manager should try some. Just mix with water and drink.

Well, Jacobs bought Pemberton's potion . . . advertised it, too . . . but sales were slow. Apparently Georgians were quite free of aches and pains that summer. That's when fate stumbled in.

The story goes that a customer came into the pharmacy one morning with a hangover. The clerk remembered Dr. Pemberton's syrup and went to mix some. He was new on the job, not yet acquainted with the procedure . . . and used carbonated water by mistake.

His mistake is still in the recipe today. Any cocaine in the original creation has long since been eliminated, so it may or may not cure your headache. The other ingredients remain basically the same.

Dr. Pemberton, the master of cures, could not cure himself. His health failed soon after that last discovery. The little business he built around it could have been bought for less than two thousand dollars when he died.

So the country druggist never shared the pot of gold at the end of what is now a rainbow of lights as wide as the world—spelling out . . . Coca-Cola!

2. THE JUGGLER

Late one afternoon, a towheaded boy of eleven stood on a kitchen chair in his Philadelphia home.

He was waiting for his father.

The boy, strong for his years, held over his head a heavy wooden box.

When Dad entered the room, the boy clobbered him.

Then, having settled accounts for a recently received spanking, the boy ran from the house to live with a friend.

His name was Claude Dukenfield, the boy who popped Pop on the noggin. And if he never again threatened his father with physical violence, it would not be the last time he wielded heavy objects.

For Claude was a juggler. One of the best of his day. If few people remember him as such, it would be his unconventional antics that detracted from an otherwise respected profession.

The antics began early in his career, as you've just read; they would not end with what appeared to be attempted patricide. For Claude, out of the recesses of his fertile imagination, had developed as a youth the perfect crime.

He found shopkeepers to be the easiest prey. Small shops protected themselves against thieves by bells that rang when the doors opened.

Claude would have a friend stand out in the street on the streetcar tracks, with his back to the car. The motorman would ding frantically at the sight of someone in his path. Then Claude would dart through the door of the shop and rob the till while the clanging of the motorman's bell drowned out the shopkeeper's.

So far as we know, he never got caught . . . and the confidence of his youth he carried into adulthood. But not as a criminal.

Claude was a juggler. A most proficient one, and that talent led to his first job: on Fortescue's Pier, in Atlantic City.

There was no admission charge to the performances at Fortescue's. The management made its profit by selling sandwiches and drinks. Claude was engaged as a juggler . . . and a drowner.

When business was bad, Claude would get into a bathing suit, wade out until the water was up to his neck, and cry for help. Saved by another employee, he would be carried back to the pier and revived to the excitement of all. A professional "drowner."

Then barkers urged sandwiches and drinks on the crowd that had gathered to watch the stirring rescue. Sometimes Claude drowned three or four times a day . . . and juggled twenty times. Few caught on.

After practicing diligently for five years, Claude became a master juggler . . . won bookings in the best vaudeville houses. He spent a large part of his early professional life abroad, playing practically every city in Europe.

He juggled his way across South Africa to the Indian Ocean, even played the South Sea Islands. For Claude by then had become supremely adept in an art that could be appreciated everywhere in the world.

In 1914, he became a Ziegfeld star and learned to combine juggling with comedy.

Then the juggling, though masterful, was phased out of his performances.

What was left was a singular *sotto voce* aside, which he swore until he died that he had learned from his mother . . . that she talked that way.

For juggling came hard, through years of practice.

Comedy came easy . . . to William Claude Dukenfield.

You knew him by his abbreviated stage name: W. C. Fields.

3. SNOW MAN

It was obvious that the big gray horse entering center ring was not a thoroughbred. But as the spotlight followed him, there was a moment of hushed silence. Accompanied by a young man, his wife, and their five small children, the steed at last turned to face the crowd.

That's when it happened. First, distant ripples of applause, then thirteen thousand spectators standing, cheering.

This was Madison Square Garden. November 1959. The National Horse Show. And if the big gray horse in center ring was an unlikely champion, there was a reason for it.

Harry de Leyer. Raised on a Netherlands farm, he married his childhood sweetheart and together they crossed the Atlantic Ocean, sought a new home in America. With only $160 between them, Harry and his new bride first tried tobacco farming in North Carolina. Then they worked on a horse farm in Pennsylvania. Harry particularly loved horses. Finally he landed the job of riding master at Knox School for Girls on Long Island, and that's where their story begins.

It was a wintry Tuesday in February when Harry returned from the horse auction. The entire De Leyer family came out to greet him . . . to see what Harry had chosen for the riding stables. When the van door opened, out came a mammoth gray-white horse. Slowly, he descended the ramp . . . stood silent, ankle-deep in a freshly fallen snow.

One of the children tugged at mother's woolen coat. "He looks just like a snow man!"

Snow Man. It was a perfect name. But the great gray horse just stood quietly, blinking in the bright winter sun . . . as though Harry and he shared some secret that made all the difference in the world.

Snow Man was trained well that season. And he was a good riding horse. But when school closed for the summer, a neighbor offered to buy him . . . offered to pay twice what Harry had paid. Reluctantly, Harry acquiesced. After all, he was in the horse business. He couldn't allow sentiment to enter into it.

As the days passed, Harry began to regret his sale. And apparently, so did Snow Man. That was when the gray gelding's hidden talent showed up, along with the horse himself. The neighbor's fences were high. Very high. But somehow, Snow Man escaped. Again and again, jumping the neighbor's fence to be reunited with the master, with the family he loved.

One day, the reunion became permanent. Harry bought back the horse, and the rest is in the record books. Winner at the Sands Point Horse Show in Long Island. Winner at the Fairfield Horse Show in Lakeville. More and more championships and important shows until the ultimate dream . . . the National at Madison Square Garden. Snow Man would be "Horse of the Year" two years running . . . but not because he ran. Snow Man was a jumper. And no one would have known, were it not for the neighbor's fence that separated a grateful animal from the master who missed him.

And Snow Man had reason to be grateful. You see, Harry arrived late at the auction, that first day they'd met. The best horses had long since been sold.

Harry and his horse shared a common destiny, and they shared a secret also—a secret that Harry had first somehow recognized through bony ribs and matted mane and sore-scarred legs.

For that great gray gelding that became the indomitable Snow Man had been rescued that day from the only other bidder, who had intended him . . . for the glue factory.

4. MAMA'S BOYS

Fellows . . . can you be too close to your mother?

From Freud to the present, the analyzers of the human mind have considered one relationship to be most important: the male with the mother figure.

When this relationship goes too far, some say, it becomes a Mother Complex.

All right. Here they are. Meet the mama's boys. . . .

Of James, it was said, there was never a more devoted son. His relationship with his mother was close . . . lasted a lifetime. What impressed James the most was his mother's unfailing confidence in him, the kind of blind confidence that only a mother can express . . . and mean it. Even on his deathbed, James's agony could only be overcome . . . by writing his mother.

Ted . . . was eternally seven. Throughout his entire life, his friends warned those about to meet him that Ted was only seven years old. Why? Well, Ted was a mama's boy. Letters to his mother began, "Darling Beloved Little Motherling." She had a compulsion for cleanliness, and so did he. Back and forth. Ted and his mother . . . were one and the same.

Now for Bill. Bill's mother put it this way: "I find that Willie needs constant watching and correcting. It requires great caution and firmness, but I do not believe we can love our children too much." You can imagine how Bill turned out.

Woody was another unashamed mama's boy, physically and emotionally clinging to his mother virtually into adulthood. There was only warmth between the two, and Woody often recalled that he came to love the best in womanhood through those apron strings.

Frank wouldn't dare go to school without his mother. And the school . . . was Harvard University. Frank's mother had an extraordinary drive for perfection, and she focused it all on Frank. For six full decades she tried to organize her son's life in minute detail . . . and Frank loved every minute of it.

Harry's mother mothered Harry quite a bit. She sat up with him countless times when he needed her. Is it any wonder that Harry returned the favor continually throughout his life? Harry's mother lived to be ninety-four and, right up to the last, there was Harry . . . conducting business matters from his mother's bedside. You see, Harry was a mama's boy too.

And what about David? When David was a big boy in the Army, he never stopped writing his mother. In fact, he once swiped a Top Secret directive to order a Mother's Day card.

All through David's life, he subconsciously imitated mama. Her laugh. Her expressions. The simplest smile.

But, then again, John imitated his mother too. They were all mama's boys. In times of crisis, it was always mother who came to mind.

So, fellows . . . can you be too close to your mother?

Well, if you can't, you might turn out like James Garfield.

Or Teddy Roosevelt.

Or William Howard Taft.

Or Woodrow Wilson.

Or Franklin Delano Roosevelt.

Or Harry S. Truman.

Or Dwight David Eisenhower.

Or John Fitzgerald Kennedy.

Even Lyndon Johnson's most cherished school paper was entitled: "I'd Rather Be Mama's Boy."

They were not afraid of their filial affection . . . and they each became President of the United States.

And if the psychologists who suspect the Mother Complex sense a reversal in the trends of greatness, well . . . have you ever heard of Lillian Carter?

Her little boy is THE REST OF THE STORY.

5. SEER SAMUEL

I don't know if you believe in ESP, but let's say you do. Let's say you believe that thought waves travel through air like radio waves . . . or that dreams can predict the future.

Every modern-day psychic and seer seems to remember the first awareness of that gift.

Edgar Cayce was a child when he began to absorb knowledge from books . . . without opening them.

Peter Hurkos' only talent was painting houses . . . until he fell off a ladder. After days of unconsciousness, he awakened to his remarkable abilities. Today, his psychic services are rendered to police departments throughout the nation . . . to aid them in the apprehension of criminals.

But this is the story of Samuel . . . a prophet's name if ever there was one. He was born under a comet . . . died under one, too. Some mystics might say that's important.

And if you're amazed by his first brush with ESP, just wait till you hear THE REST OF THE STORY.

Seer Samuel was not born in Tibet, but in Florida.

His young life, though exciting to him, was not extraordinary . . . until one night. The night he had a dream.

Samuel's brother Henry had shipped out on the *Pennsylvania*. One day, the ship's captain swore at brother Henry and struck him. As is the inclination of older brothers, Samuel went on board after hearing of the incident and decked Henry's assailant.

Yes, Samuel was quite protective, quite fond of his brother Henry. So much so that his hatred for the *Pennsylvania*'s captain survived that impulsive retaliation.

Perhaps his mind was there . . . that night at his sister's house . . . the night he had a dream.

No sooner had Samuel fallen into slumber than a picture welled up before his closed eyes . . . a dreadful picture.

It was a corpse in a coffin . . . a metallic coffin, supported by two chairs.

Half wanting to know, half not wanting to know, Samuel, in his dream slowly approached the coffin.

At his bedside one might have heard Samuel cry out as he turned away, still dreaming, from the sight.

For the corpse . . . in that coffin of metal . . . was Henry, his brother. And on Henry's breast . . . a red rose.

Samuel awakened with a start, sat upright in bed. Tears kissed the darkness as he fumbled for the light, got up, and went to awaken his sister.

He told her everything. About the coffin of metal. About the two chairs. About the red rose. And about . . . Henry.

It was just a bad dream, his sister assured him. And they would both forget about it . . . until one sultry mid-June morning. . . .

The *Pennsylvania* was docked, was loading wood . . . when four of her eight boilers exploded.

The *Pennsylvania*.

Henry's ship.

Her front end was blown away, and in a disaster comparable to a jet-plane crash today, a hundred and fifty lives were lost.

Brother Henry was among the less fortunate who lingered and, scalded beyond recovery, suffered terribly for six days.

Each of those days and nights, Samuel sat beside him. When it was over, for the first time in almost a week, he slept.

The next day, Samuel went to the room where the bodies of the dead awaited burial. Each in a coffin of unpainted wood.

Except one.

Those who held deathwatch with Samuel had so admired the gentle, gallant young Henry, who had suffered so . . . that they had collected sixty dollars and bought for him a metallic casket. It sat supported on two chairs.

As Samuel stood beside his brother, seeing that awful dream materialize in every detail but one . . . an elderly lady entered the room and placed on the breast of the dead brother . . . one red rose.

Now, whether Samuel was really a seer, I'll leave up to you.

But if dreams of the future continued to come true, that side of his life has been obscured by a perhaps greater gift.

For seer Samuel, born under a comet, was born in Florida . . . Florida, Missouri.

The steamship *Pennsylvania* . . . was a riverboat.

And the lad who had that bad dream come true, Samuel Clemens, you know . . . as Mark Twain.

6. THE MOUSE THAT ROARED

Steve Morris was not a typical child. But when you're nine years old, the desire to be typical is very strong.

Steve was born in Saginaw, Michigan. When he was very young, his folks moved to Detroit, to a little apartment on Hastings Street.

Of all the people and things Steve has since forgotten and remembered from those early years, one woman stands out in his mind. One woman encouraged him and gave him the courage to be extraordinary. Steve's elementary-school teacher, Mrs. Beneduci.

Of course, Mrs. Beneduci was a wise woman. She realized that mere words, to a nine-year-old, might not carry much weight. With the unwitting aid of a little gray mouse she seized instead upon a particular opportunity, and from that day on Steve knew his greatest pride, the calling of a life.

It happened in a tiny grade-school classroom in Detroit, THE REST OF THE STORY.

Mrs. Beneduci called her class to order.

"Come now! Jesse! Annette! Settle down, people . . . we're going to open with history today. . . ."

The little ones squirmed in their seats, suppressing the nervous giggles of infant inmates wishing to be sprung.

"I know you'd rather be outside playing," said Mrs. Beneduci. "It's a lovely day. But if you learn nothing in life, all you'll ever know how to do is play!"

The teacher gave a sympathetic half-smile.

Young Steve Morris was quiet.

"Amy," asked Mrs. Beneduci, "who was Abraham Lincoln?"

Amy stared at her desk. "Uh . . . he, uh, had a beard."

The class collapsed with laughter.

"Steve Morris?" said the teacher. "Same question."

"He was the sixteenth President of the United States," came the answer. Solidly. Without hesitation.

The class was silent once more.

Steve's problem was not the answers. He had them all. In fact, little Steve Morris also had a rather remarkable gift. But answers to questions would mean nothing in themselves, unless Steve could be made to realize just how important that gift really was.

"All right," Mrs. Beneduci continued, "Abraham Lincoln was our sixteenth President. He was President during the Civil War—"

Then she stopped, as though she were listening to something. "What's that?" asked the teacher, half to herself. "Who's making that noise?"

The puzzled classmates looked at each other. Steve sat quietly.

"I hear something like scratching . . . it's very faint," said Mrs. Beneduci. "It sounds . . . it sounds like a mouse!"

The little girls screamed. Some stood on their chairs with the speed of ascending lightning.

"Calm down, everyone," said the teacher. "It's nothing to get excited about. Steve, will you help me find the poor little creature?"

Steve sat straight upright in his chair, brightening considerably. "OK," he said. "Now everybody be quiet!"

In the sudden stillness Steve cocked his head, hesitated for a moment, and pointed slowly to the wastebasket.

"He's right over there!" said Steve proudly. "I can hear him!"

And so he was, a frightened little gray mouse that had been rummaging beneath the wastepaper, hoping to go undiscovered.

But he had been discovered by little Steve Morris, whom nature had given a remarkable pair of ears in compensation for having denied him eyes since birth.

So the class settled back to business. And the little gray mouse became a mascot. In the heart of small, unsighted Steve, a pride was born . . . and that pride is with him still.

After the incident, Mrs. Beneduci would continue to encourage the talent that the whole world now knows and respects, and she always reminded Steve of the little gray mouse that once made its home in a wastebasket . . . by accident?

In time, the marvelous ears of Steve Morris gave popular music something to be proud of . . . a singer-composer-musician-producer with five Grammys in '75 . . . seventeen gold singles . . . four gold albums . . . four platinum records.

For, once upon a time, a little gray mouse roared . . . gave a small boy confidence in what nature had given him. And Steve Morris, from the time he was ten . . . for his gifted ears . . . was never known as anything . . . but Little Stevie Wonder.

7. THE FRAME

Now I'm going to tell you a mystery story. A real-life mystery story. But I'm going to tell you first how it ends. It's important that you know, so you can keep the facts straight.

The Colonel was married. And he also had a mistress.

Indeed the Colonel was just about to leave his wife for the other woman, when his wife decided to kill him.

All right, do you have this? It's important.

The Colonel's wife wants to do away with her husband . . . so she conceives . . . the perfect crime!

The wife will make it appear as though her husband, the Colonel, has murdered *her*. The authorities would do the rest.

The Colonel would be tried, convicted, executed; his wife could turn up later . . . with feigned amnesia.

The perfect crime, right?

And, mystery buffs, please don't feel cheated because you know more than you should. Despite all that you've heard, you'd never guess THE REST OF THE STORY.

One frosty night in December of 1926, a car was found at the bottom of a chalk pit in Newlands Corner, England.

Inside the car was a fur coat belonging to the Colonel's wife. The woman had disappeared. And the police . . . suspected murder.

The Colonel himself was interrogated first. Where had he been on the night in question?

Well, the Colonel explained, he'd been at a dinner party.

What was the occasion?

The Colonel appeared embarrassed. The dinner party was for himself and his lady. They were going to announce their engagement.

The detectives looked at each other. Was the Colonel at the party all evening?

No. He had received a telephone call from his wife. She had heard what was going on and was about to come to the party to make a scene. Naturally, the Colonel had to go home for a while, to calm his wife.

Did he?

Yes, the Colonel had gone home. No one was there and he had returned to the party.

Had the Colonel and his wife been on good terms prior to her disappearance?

Yes. Well, no. Not exactly. They'd had their disagreements. In fact, they'd had quite a row the morning before the dinner party. About the Colonel's "lady."

If the detectives prejudged the Colonel guilty, you can imagine why. His testimony was incriminating.

Meanwhile, a force of two thousand was organized to search a forty-square-mile area for the missing body. The authorities dragged a deep water hole near the chalk pit where her car was found. Tracking dogs and light planes scoured the area.

Publicity mounted steadily. The London newspapers were calling the incident The Crime of the Century. The *Daily News* offered one hundred pounds for any information leading to the solution of the mystery.

And who is being asked not to leave town?

The Colonel, of course. Obvious motive. The mistress involvement. And no alibi.

Of course, you know he didn't do it. You know his wife was hiding out, waiting for her husband to be convicted of murder and sent to the gallows. You know, because I told you.

But there's something you didn't know.

The Colonel's wife had planned everything. She'd left the ignition key off when she pushed her car into the pit, so the police would know that it was pushed and not driven. She had even left a fur coat in the car. It was very cold that night, remember?

When investigators would find the coat, they would not suspect she had left the scene herself.

Yes, the Colonel's wife had figured it all out . . . except for one thing: There was no place for her to hide!

Twelve days after her disappearance, her famous face was recognized on the other side of England.

Not only was the Colonel's wife well known but she, of all people, should have been able to get away with murder!

For the Colonel's wife . . . the real-life almost-murderess . . . was the author of fiction's most successful whodunits. She was the Mistress of Mystery . . . Agatha Christie.

8. FOR LOVE OF JIM

Jack and Jim were the best of friends. Devoted. Inseparable.

So when Jim lost both his legs in a railroad accident, Jack did everything he could to help.

At first, Jim was certain his career with the railroad was finished. Then the company gave him another job . . . as a signalman. His outpost was to be a lonely little stop, more than two hundred miles from anywhere.

Jack went along to be whatever help he could be on the new job. Anything he could to help his crippled friend.

But the lengths of self-sacrifice to which Jack was willing to go are THE REST OF THE STORY.

Jim had come out of the hospital with no legs. He'd barely recovered from the trauma of a double amputation when the railroad had given him the new assignment.

Jim would live in a little wooden shack about a hundred and fifty yards from the signal tower. It was going to be lonely out there. And there would be myriad difficulties and adjustments.

But Jack would help, for a while anyway. It was hoped, for long enough for Jim to overcome those initial difficulties and make those first adjustments.

In the beginning, Jack stuck around mostly for company. He swept out the shack and pumped water from the well and tended the garden and made himself useful in all the ways legless Jim could not.

There was a little trolley, a single-seater that led from the shack to the signal tower. Jack pushed Jim on that trolley several times a day and stood there while Jim operated the big levers in sequence. And, eventually, Jack got so familiar with Jim's schedule that he began to walk out and operate the signal system himself.

Sure enough, pretty soon, in addition to housecleaning and the rest, Jack gradually began to take over all these duties for the railroad . . . though officially he was not an employee!

There was a lot to remember on that job, a lot to be done. If a "point" had to be adjusted farther up the line, Jack would have to listen for a passing engine, flag him down, and give him a special key to make the adjustment.

Daily responsibilities at the signal tower included working the levers that set the signals, as well as the tower controls that opened and closed siding switches.

There was a lot going on at the lonely little outpost, and soon Jack was doing all the work. But he never complained. After all, Jim was his friend. Jim had just gone through a terrible ordeal. It was the least Jack could do . . . for a while, anyway.

But a while turned to weeks, and weeks turned to months, and months turned to years.

For more than nine years Jack kept house for Jim. Jack pumped water from the well, tended the garden, trudged out to the signal tower each day to operate the heavy equipment.

Until one day, after a bout with tuberculosis, Jack died.

But in all those years, Jack, who had never before worked on the railroad . . . Jack, who had never before seen a signal tower in his life . . . never made a mistake.

In nine years, he never threw a switch incorrectly . . . he never sided a car in error. In nine years, there was not one accident or even a narrow miss on the Port Elizabeth main line . . . because of Jack.

Jack is buried in Cape Colony, South Africa, not far from the outpost where he worked for almost a decade . . . for his love of his friend. His grave is a silent testament to selflessness.

And I don't think I mentioned that Jack . . . the friend who cleaned house and pumped water and tended garden and manned the switch tower that ran the railroad . . . was not a man at all. He was . . . a baboon.

9.   CHAINS

It was in a little colonial house in eastern Virginia . . . that Henry lived . . . apparently alone.

One late evening, friends came to visit. Henry and his guests sat in the candlelit parlor, quietly talking, watching the flickering shadows on the walls. There was a lull in the conversation . . . and a noise!

Faint at first, then louder.

A scratching sound . . . beneath the floor.

Everyone had heard it. Henry . . . pretended not to.

There were lighthearted remarks about ghosts and such, and after a minute or so, Henry stretched, yawned, asked to be excused so that he might retire for the night.

When his visitors had gone, Henry tugged at his collar, sighing. He was alone again. And none too soon.

For as Henry's friends rode off into the dark, against the fading counterpoint of their horses' hoofs . . . another noise. Like the first. Followed by the sound of dragging along the floor joists beneath Henry's feet.

Henry stiffened, silently regarding the inconspicuous trapdoor in the hallway floor.

He reached for a lantern, approached the secret entrance, bent down, took hold of the smooth iron ring . . . and pulled the false panel away.

Henry peered into the gaping blackness, lowering his lantern, then himself, into the cold cellar.

As the kerosene flame cast a soft yellow light all about, there was a rustling in the corner. A figure, barely visible through the gloom, cringing in terror of the brightness, waited.

Henry walked toward it.

Henry lifted the lantern . . . and the light fell directly . . . upon a face! A horribly animated countenance with twisted features which snarled one moment and wept the next. A blanched wild-eyed visage, filled with torment. The face . . . of Henry's wife.

Henry could not recall the duration of her madness, nor could he recount the endless procession of days and months he had descended the cellar stairs to feed and to care for her. All the hours of Henry's life had by now blended into one solitary hour of despair.

For Henry, the anguish had not diminished . . . to watch his wife tug against her straitjacket restraints . . . to see his love imprisoned through no wrong of her own.

Once in a great while, like the pulsing glow of a near-cold ember, the faint reflection of a happiness long past shone in the beleaguered woman's face. And then, like a flash of black lightning, the horror would return.

These were the visions that stalked Henry from the depths of that secret place . . . the waking dreams he took to bed with him at night, and at morning into the warm sun.

Was this on his mind? Did those visions haunt him, as he addressed the assembly at St. John's Church the next day, March 23, 1775? These were his words:

"Shall we try argument? . . . Shall we resort to entreaty? . . . What terms shall we find which have not been already exhausted? . . . We have petitioned, we have remonstrated, we have supplicated. . . . We have been spurned with contempt. . . . There is no longer any room for hope. . . . Is life so dear or peace so sweet as to be purchased at the price of chains? . . . Forbid it, Almighty God! . . . I know not what course others may take, but as for me, give me liberty or give me death!"

Patrick Henry.

And now you know THE REST OF THE STORY.

10. BANNED IN BOSTON

From Puritan times to the twentieth century, "banned in Boston" has been a much-sought-after stigma.

An author whose work was banned in Boston was most certain to reap a bountiful literary harvest almost everywhere else.

And so it was for the brilliant renegade playwright Eugene O'Neill.

Eugene O'Neill.

Some call him "the father of American drama." His mammoth play *Strange Interlude* was scheduled for Boston in 1929, but it was banned. And because it was, O'Neill's play and his innovator reputation flourished.

A small-time restaurant owner also prospered from O'Neill's exile, and that is THE REST OF THE STORY.

Strange Interlude.

It played New York in 1928.

The drama was filled with para-Freudian overtones. The text and context were new, naughty, riddled with guilt feelings, promiscuity, latent homosexuality, insanity, adultery, abortion, illegitimacy, neurotic motherhood, and incestuous desire.

In short, Eugene O'Neill had staged "Mary Hartman, Mary Hartman" nearly fifty years ahead of time.

When you look at *Strange Interlude* objectively, from today's point of view, the O'Neill semiclassic is somewhat of a soap opera, hypermelodramatic, contrived.

New Yorkers took it all in stride. Broadway audiences, though fascinated, were still blasé, so the play needed a shot in the arm.

Strange Interlude, due for Boston, was banned.

Boston's mayor, admittedly and unashamedly having never seen the O'Neill drama, condemned it as "an affront to public decency."

That was just the sort of publicity *Strange Interlude* required to turn big box office. The play opened in nearby Quincy, Massachusetts, and the affronted public showed up in droves, flocking to see the salacious material that had caused all the fuss.

Now, keep in mind that *Strange Interlude* is a little more than four solid hours of drama. Nine acts, four hours. So the producers scheduled a dinner intermission . . . a break in the play long enough for the audience to go out and enjoy an evening meal.

Across the street from the theater in Quincy where *Strange Interlude* was playing, there was a little restaurant. The owner had been doing passable business but nothing to speak of, until O'Neill's lengthy production came to town.

Virtually overnight, the modest restaurateur watched his business boom, his cash-register tills overflow. Every evening at intermission time, crowds of theatergoers formed a line at the door of the little establishment, and everyone was happy.

Then *Strange Interlude* came to the end of its run. Playwright O'Neill went on to bigger and better plays. The theater in Quincy fell back to less controversial productions. And the little restaurant across the street resumed its business as usual.

And the depression came.

But while other businesses failed, the little restaurant in Quincy hung on and eventually prospered beyond the wildest dreams of its modest owner.

Because thousands of people, many distinguished or influential or just plain hungry, had come to Quincy to see a play banned in Boston, the little eating place across the street was remembered and continually patronized. It flourished.

After the depression, the owner expanded and the business bearing his name eventually became an American household word.

By 1935, there were twenty-five all over Massachusetts. By 1940, there were more than a hundred . . . and the chain dangled down the Atlantic coast to Florida.

Today, there are a thousand. From Maine to California. The chain has forged itself into a nationwide symbol because, once upon a time, curious crowds came to Quincy to see how naughty was O'Neill.

Even then, the owner's name hung over the window of the little restaurant across the street. His name . . . Howard Johnson.

11. THE KIDNAPING OF "BAB"

Of late, Italy has become the kidnap capital of the world.

Spurred by international attention to the Getty case, Italy's kidnap crime wave steadily mounted to include victims of every stature, wide-ranging ransoms, criminals with a variety of motives.

I'm going to relate now what might seem to be just another one of Italy's many kidnap plots. Then I'll tell you THE REST OF THE STORY.

His real name was Billy.

His parents called him "Bab."

Bab. A pet name, short for Baby.

Bab was the infant son of a renowned British novelist. The family had been on tour, had only recently come to visit Naples, in sunny southern Italy.

Bab's mother was a fresh-air fanatic. Her prime consideration, wherever the family went, was the quality of the environment for her children.

While in Italy, it was nonetheless emphasized. Bab's nurse would take the child on regular outings for fresh air and sunshine.

I mention this to point up the predictability of Bab's daily schedule. Every afternoon at the same time, Bab and his nurse could be found, in the park, by the same light, sand-colored wall.

So it was on one particular afternoon . . . when two immaculately dressed gentlemen approached Bab's nurse, claiming they had been sent by Bab's father to fetch the child.

When the nurse offered to return Bab herself, one of the men snatched the two-year-old boy from her arms. Both kidnapers got away.

Within twenty-four hours, Bab's parents were notified. The infant was indeed being held for ransom. The amount was equivalent in American currency to a hundred and twenty-five dollars! That's all . . . one hundred and twenty-five dollars ransom for the boy's safe return. As Bab's parents quickly arranged to meet the kidnapers' demand, investigators put their heads together, trying to make sense out of it.

At last it was agreed that the kidnapers merely wanted attention, notoriety for the sake of it. With nothing more than this to go on, it was not until Bab was returned unharmed to his parents that authorities discovered the kidnapers' mountain hideout.

Vacant.

Bab's story had a happier ending than many. His captors had not been sadists, nor had they been political terrorists. In all probability they were just small-time crooks.

But if the rising international crime rate is what disturbs you most about this case . . . you would perhaps be interested to know that Bab, the infant son of a celebrated English writer, was kidnaped in '39 . . . 1839.

Bab's childhood, from then on, was healthy and normal. He grew up to become a fine young man, first a lawyer, then a writer —like his dad.

His first literary efforts were written under the pen name "Bab" . . . until he met another gentleman with whom he would collaborate on more than a dozen unforgettable stage works.

Two of those works included the kidnaping Bab claimed to recall. But you remember Bab for his facetiously witty rhymes, for his capricious librettos to the world's best-loved comic operas.

For Bab, the infant who was once spirited away and ransomed for a hundred and twenty-five dollars . . . grew up to satirize his childhood misfortune in *The Gondoliers* and *H.M.S. Pinafore.*

Bab was Sir William S. Gilbert . . . one half of the most remarkable Gilbert and Sullivan.

12. FALL WHERE THEY MAY

If Neil Vanderbilt was spoiled . . . he could afford to be.

The son of a Staten Island farmer, Neil had clawed his way to the top. Built from scratch one of the most remarkable transportation empires the world has ever seen.

So if Neil Vanderbilt was spoiled, he could afford to be finicky . . . to have his way.

Cornelius Vanderbilt. Born not twenty years after the Declaration of Independence.

A stubborn child, Neil refused to attend school past the age of eleven. At sixteen, he'd purchased a small sailboat with money borrowed from his parents. But the vessel was not for pleasure. Not entirely. Young Neil used it to carry passengers between Staten Island and New York City. A lifetime of enterprise was just beginning.

During the War of 1812, Neil was authorized to transport provisions and soon had a small fleet engaged in river and coastal trade. In 1818, he sold out . . . went to work for shipping magnate Thomas Gibbons. By 1829, Vanderbilt had formed his own steamboat company, managing to dominate the business with lower fares and greater luxury. In a short while, his lines extended to Boston and to Providence and, by 1846, "Commodore" Cornelius Vanderbilt was a millionaire.

During the 1850s he frequented a little place in Saratoga Springs, New York, called Moon Lake Lodge. Saratoga Springs was a resort town catering to the pre-Kitty Hawk jet set, you might say, and Moon Lake Lodge was their smartest restaurant . . . the talk of the town.

You'd expect the chef at Moon Lake to have been imported from Paris, but George Crum was a full-fledged, honest-to-goodness Indian chief.

And though "chief" chef Crum was schooled in international cuisine, he couldn't be expected to know all the new recipes being created.

Probably that's how the latest culinary rage from France escaped him. This delicacy, a favorite of the elite, was called "French Fries." French Fried Potatoes in those days were very French, relatively new, exotic, exclusive.

That is how Moon Lake's most distinguished customer comes in: transportation tycoon Cornelius Vanderbilt. He, too, was quite familiar with international cuisine and decided one evening to order a plate of French Fries. When they were brought to him, Cornelius complained that French Fried Potatoes were sliced much thinner in Paris. He'd just returned from Paris and he knew! "These," he told the waiter, "are much too thick!"

Dutifully the waiter returned the potatoes to the kitchen.

Busy chef George Crum thought little of it. Working at Moon Lake Lodge, he was not unaccustomed to the sometimes petulance of the well-to-do. George proceeded to slice and prepare another batch of French Fries, thinner this time.

But shortly after the plate left the kitchen, it was back again. "They're still too thick," the waiter told the chef.

That did it.

Now, this was 1853. Two subordinates were attempting to wrest control of the company from Vanderbilt. It had not been an easy year. Or perhaps there was some other irritation that evening.

Whatever the case, chef George Crum had had enough. With an I'll-fix-him look in his eye, George sharpened his knife to a razor edge, seized a potato, and began slicing it paper thin. He then dipped the slices into boiling fat, salted them to excess, and personally bolted through the kitchen door with the plate of brown, brittle shavings.

The waiters tried to stop him, but it was too late. George had made it to the Vanderbilt table with what appeared a most overdone, oversalted, and unpalatable offering. Neil liked it! At least he said so. Maybe he just felt guilty about having complained so vigorously, but Commodore Cornelius Vanderbilt said he liked it and that was enough endorsement to win for this dish a permanent place on the prestigious menu of the Saratoga inn.

The American variation of what the French called fries. By 1887 the recipe was in the White House cookbook, and after potato peeling and slicing were automated in the mid twenties . . . chef Crum's innovation was available and wanted world-wide.

Cornelius Vanderbilt's transportation empire served him well. But the tasty legacy he left us . . . the by-product of his moment of petulance in 1853 . . . the overcooked revenge of an overwrought chef . . . was the potato chip.

Everybody has a favorite teacher.

Artie Doyle had a favorite teacher.

Artie Doyle was a medical student. First year med school, he had a favorite teacher . . . a professor named Bell.

Dr. Bell must have been a fascinating instructor, because Artie remembered him all his life. In fact, that's how we know about Dr. Bell. From Artie.

The thing that made Dr. Joseph Bell so interesting was the way he taught. It was so special that he kept students on the edge of their seats.

Joseph Bell had started at the bottom as a hospital attendant and wound up head of the Edinburgh University medical school.

If you knew Dr. Bell, you'd say he made it because he knew *how* to think. That's what he was always telling his students: You've got to learn *how* to think or all you know won't get you anywhere.

Bell used to demonstrate this to his students. He had an outpatient facility where he interviewed patients, and sometimes he would invite his class to join him there. He'd have them stand around and watch while these new patients came in to see the doctor.

The stories make Bell sound a lot like Dr. Gillespie, squinting over his glasses and intimidating his patients with a childishly wicked expression.

Then he'd say something like, "Oh, you must be either a cork cutter or a slater!" The startled patient would acknowledge that he was, in fact, a slater. Dr. Bell would then turn to his class and wink. He had observed a slight callus on one side of the forefinger and a little thickening on the outside of the thumb. For observant Bell that was enough to identify the trade of his patient.

Another time, Dr. Bell turned to his class immediately before interviewing a patient. "This man's a cobbler," he told them. And he was right. Bell had caught a glimpse of the man's trousers. They were worn at the inside of the knee . . . right where the cobbler's lapstone sits.

Now, you say this doesn't sound much like medicine. But what Dr. Bell was trying to impress upon his students . . . what he was trying to cultivate in them . . . was the power of observation. You must notice *everything*, he told them. A good doctor has to notice *everything!*

Still another time, Dr. Bell told a brand-new patient that he, the patient, was not long discharged from the Army. Bell had no readily obvious way of knowing this. The man was wearing street clothes. But Dr. Bell went on to say that the patient had been a non-com officer in a Highland regiment, and that he had been stationed at Barbados!

Dr. Bell was right on all counts. It was very simple, he explained to his students. The man was respectful but did not remove his hat. They do not in the Army; but he would have learned civilian ways had he been long discharged. He had an air of authority, was obviously Scottish. As to Barbados, his complaint was elephantiasis, which is West Indian and not British.

And to Dr. Bell's students, something else was obvious . . . that for Dr. Bell medicine was sort of, well . . . detective work. It's not a matter of coincidence that complicated mystery stories also fascinated him.

So it was the way he thought and the way he taught that kept his students spellbound. I'm thinking, however, about Artie Doyle, the first-year med student who sat enraptured in the back of Bell's class.

Artie would go on to become a doctor. Yet you will know him better for another talent.

Artie also became a writer . . . and though the medicine he learned from Dr. Bell was significant, his professor's power of inductive reasoning was even more so.

Artie immortalized it, and him, in a character the world can never forget. Because Artie one day became *Sir* Arthur. Sir Arthur Conan Doyle.

And because one classmate remembered him so well . . . Dr. Bell is even yet alive and well . . . a hundred years later and living in literary history forever as the greatest-ever criminal diagnostician.

It was Dr. Bell who was the author's model for the master sleuth of all time . . . Sherlock Holmes.

14. PEN PALS

Philology is the study of literature literally. It's the study of whole texts and single words and the meanings of each.

Is it any wonder that when The Macmillan Company was shopping around for someone to edit a brand-new dictionary . . . they chose Dr. James Murray, president of the Philological Society in England?

Dr. Murray had quite established himself in philological studies. He was the best. But the task would be an enormous one.

You already know what is now considered his crowning achievement: the great Oxford dictionary.

Cawdrey's was the first English dictionary, 1604, a mere few pages compared to the completed Oxford dictionary of 1933. The latter took over half a century to be assembled . . . more than half a century and more than fifteen thousand pages. It should not come as a surprise, then, that its first and foremost editor, Dr. James Murray, needed all the help he could get.

Among those who were the greatest help was Dr. W. C. Minors. He was Dr. Murray's pen pal, although these two learned men had never met.

It seems Dr. W. C. Minors had heard that the great Oxford dictionary was being compiled. The thought fascinated him.

Might he be of any assistance? he wrote Dr. Murray.

At first, Dr. Murray was amused by the offer from this unknown scholar. He knew that good lexicographers are born and
not made. It takes a particular kind of mind, and who *was* this
Dr. Minors anyway? But Dr. Murray wrote a letter of thanks to
Dr. Minors saying, yes, he'd be interested in any suggestions. He
wasn't really.

The next letter from Dr. Minors was a shocker . . . dozens of
items, definitions, references . . . each expertly arranged and constructed in every detail . . . and more than that. Immediately, Dr.
Murray was convinced that he was corresponding with a genius.

Quickly Dr. Murray dashed off a letter expressing his extreme
gratitude. He'd had no idea how unusually qualified Dr. Minors
was . . . and he'd be honored to accept any further guidance, or
criticism, or aid whatsoever from this great mind.

Dr. Minors complied.

Before long the letters Dr. Murray received from Dr. Minors
numbered in the thousands! Thousands of letters containing thousands of valuable items that eventually found their way into the
great Oxford dictionary.

Finally Dr. Murray could bear it no longer. He'd been respectful of Dr. Minors' privacy, all the while knowing no more about
this mystery scholar than his address: Dr. W. C. Minors, Crowthorne, England.

But now it was time they should meet. So Dr. Murray wrote
Dr. Minors, inviting him to be the guest of Oxford University for
a week.

The letter Dr. Murray received in answer was a curious one. In
it Dr. Minors said that he was, for physical reasons, forced to decline the invitation. He would, however, be delighted to have Dr.
Murray visit him at Crowthorne.

Dr. Murray accepted.

In a few days he traveled to Wellington College Station, where
he was met by a liveried coachman.

"Dr. Murray?" the coachman asked, "I've been instructed to
take you to Dr. Minors."

Without another word they were on their way to Dr. Minors'
residence and to the most remarkable revelation of Dr. Murray's
life.

For the great mind of Dr. Minors . . . the brilliant brain behind a major contribution to the great Oxford dictionary . . . was only partly there.

After that one unforgettable meeting between the two scholars, they never met again.

For you see, though this extraordinary man's love of learning could not be constrained, he had to be. Dr. Minors was a convicted mad-dog murderer.

Dr. Murray's pen pal . . . was in the pen . . . an inmate at the Broadmoore Asylum for the Criminally Insane!

15. THE NIGHT SIN CITY DIED

It's been called the greatest single tragedy in the history of that great midwestern state.

October 8, 1871. The night the "wicked" city to the north . . . burned down. More than fifteen hundred people lost their lives as fiery tongues lapped at the waters of Lake Michigan.

A portrait of the northern midwest in 1871 might well have been described as a desert with gently shifting seasons. From the late winter, all through that long, torrid summer . . . virtually bone-dry.

A light shower on September 5 kissed the parched earth like an eyedropper squeezed into a frying pan. And then . . . nothing. The entire state cringed helplessly under nature's blowtorch.

And the city to the north . . . was waiting. How odd! Lake Michigan, a fresh-water ocean, sleeping at her elbow to the east. And the long, languid river snaking its way through the heart of town.

Water everywhere . . . except where it counted. Water all around, mocking destiny. And the unsuspecting city to the north . . . was waiting.

October 7. Saturday. Hotel transients talked about the weather. Railroad men, about their shipments. Theatergoers, about the play tonight.

A forgotten line from a newspaper editorial said, "Unless we have rain, only God knows how soon a conflagration may sweep this town."

But Saturday passed, on Sunday the holocaust began raging.

The mighty roar of the flames in the dead of night was most terrible to hear, said those who lived to recall. A heat so intense the very earth seemed to melt like butter. Beneath the towering crimson, pale-yellow and white, men ran like ants for the river.

The bridges ablaze, some lifted their heads from watery cover to inhale pure fire. With the sky a ghostly, ghastly midnight sun, the night waned slowly.

When the devilish rhapsody of flames and screams subsided, the city was almost dead.

Some said she paid for her sins . . . like Sodom, more than two thousand years before. True, the Saturday night joints, jam-packed with the drunken, the senseless, the incoherent, the unsuspecting . . . could have appeared like live bait in some moralist's metaphor. But you know the truth. Or at least, most of it.

What you may not know was the name of the city whose demise you've just relived: Peshtigo, Wisconsin.

You'd probably not heard of the Great Peshtigo Fire because of a simultaneous tragedy. For while fifteen hundred lost their lives in Peshtigo, publicity favored another fire on that very same night . . . in which three hundred died.

The other fire, in a city to the south, you know a great deal about. The Great *Chicago* Fire.

And now you know THE REST OF THE STORY.

16. THE MUSIC THAT MADE HIM CRY

Every Sunday night, Rachmaninoff cried.

Brilliant composer, conductor, pianist, Sergei Rachmaninoff.

Despite the dour expression his public saw, he was not an unpleasant fellow.

And yet, every Sunday night . . . he cried.

Rachmaninoff's career took him down many musical avenues. And it's interesting to note that pianist Rachmaninoff was especially fond of the violin. His joint recitals with violinist Fritz Kreisler were legendary. Many recordings of their work together survive them.

But there was one violinist with whom the great Sergei Rachmaninoff would never play. It was his music that made the composer cry.

You see, radio broadcast concerts were not uncommon in that day. Conductor Toscanini gave them. And pianist Horowitz. And Rachmaninoff himself.

So whenever the composer's favorite violinist graced the air waves with his magical music, Rachmaninoff was there, a devoted fan, listening attentively . . . and then he would cry.

Why . . . is THE REST OF THE STORY.

It stands to reason that Rachmaninoff's favorite violinist was a fellow Russian. American-born, of Russian parents.

And the two had much more in common than their heritage.

As children, both loved their chosen instrument but neither liked to practice . . . and for a surprisingly long time, neither of these great artists played their instruments well.

Both backgrounds were disciplinarian, and yet neither boy could resist playing hooky from school.

Both, while adoring classical music, enjoyed popular music from time to time . . . even played it once in a while.

Their mothers set their earliest musical examples. Both played the piano. But neither child had much else in common with their parents. It was their maternal grandmothers to whom they related best.

Neither boy was by any means small in stature, but both would run from a fight.

Both were to marry once . . . for life. And both wives survived them.

Both seemed to resist old age, though they eventually reached it.

And both, though they rarely smiled before their public, possessed a remarkable . . . if dry . . . sense of humor.

Rachmaninoff? Humor?

Violinist Fritz Kreisler remembered a prankish Rachmaninoff. . . .

It was during one of their joint recitals in New York that Kreisler had a momentary lapse of memory. He edged toward the piano and whispered to Rachmaninoff, "Where are we?" Rachmaninoff never skipped a note as he answered, "In Carnegie Hall!"

Yes, the composer had a sense of humor. In fact, it was that sense of humor that brought him and his favorite violinist together.

Though that great violinist was not the incomparable Kreisler, with whom Rachmaninoff played, he was a great artist indeed . . . and Rachmaninoff was his greatest fan.

For the tears Rachmaninoff cried when he listened to him . . . were tears of laughter.

The music that made the composer weep for joy . . . was humor itself.

And while, for all their similarities, Rachmaninoff went on to achieve musical immortality, violinist Benjamin Kubelsky did not. The would-be violinist would take another path to the admiration of the great Rachmaninoff . . . and achieve immortality elsewhere for himself.

If, at last, Kubelsky would be recognized as he played his simple theme song "Love in Bloom," it was enough for the world . . . and for composer Rachmaninoff.

For the unspectacular violinist who scratched and screeched his way into the hearts of those who knew how to play, you know . . . as Jack Benny.

17. MURDER AT TOBAGO

In the shallows off the coast of Trinidad . . . where the turquoise Caribbean and the mighty Atlantic meet . . . standing guard by the graceful Antillean tail . . . is Tobago.

Lush, torrid Tobago. Target south for West Indian trade. Two hundred years ago.

The story is there and then . . . of mutiny and murder . . . and the Scottish sea captain who fled for his life. His case, never tried, is history's to decide. But the place to which he came, his assumed name and subsequent fame, constitute THE REST OF THE STORY.

For Captain Paul there was only the sea. Cabin boy on a merchant ship at twelve, his own command at twenty-two. The waters were calm for a young boy and his dreams; they grew turbulent, menacing, for the young man.

Round trip to the West Indies was a long haul. Scottish merchant vessels, tiny by modern standards, were human pressure cookers . . . volatile floating warehouses for people as well as their cargo. While discipline and respect were difficult to maintain, they were especially so for a youthful ship's master. Trouble seemed inevitable. And the inevitable came. At Tobago.

Record of the incident comes from Captain Paul's letter to a friend, so we'll see it as he saw it.

There was mutiny in the air from the very start. One crew

member, whom Captain Paul refers to as "the ringleader," had done everything in his power to disquiet the others on the outward passage. Now they were docked at Tobago. The ringleader, seizing the opportunity to create further unrest, demanded advance payment for the entire crew.

That was impossible, Captain Paul argued. Cash on hand was needed to invest in a return cargo. The men would be paid when they reached home.

It was not good enough. The ringleader, a hulking brute of a man, threatened the young ship's master . . . forced him to take refuge below deck. It was there, in the darkness, that Captain Paul would have to decide. He had run, but captains cannot run. The question was not of age or size or strength. It was a matter of responsibility, of sworn duty.

With a trembling hand, the twenty-six-year-young captain drew his sword and emerged into the sunlight. For a single, breathless moment, the stunned mutineers stood their ground. Their ringleader, not about to be intimidated by a mere boy, reached for a bludgeon and charged him. Roaring threats, he swung the weapon back and high against a pale tropical sky. That's when Captain Paul . . . ran him through.

At once, the air was still. A man lay dead upon the deck. The mutiny had come to a shocking end. Solemnly, the ship's master prepared to give himself up, amid protests from his second in command. He couldn't give himself up. Not here. Not in Tobago. There was no authority to try an admiralty case and his life would be in danger if he stood a jury trial in their civil court. He must flee the Caribbean . . . north, to the continent of America. To the British colonies there. He must change his name . . . begin a new life. He was good to no one as a hanged man.

Reluctantly, Captain Paul relinquished his command. Many months of flight would bring him to many ports . . . a man without a nation or a name . . . until he finally reached Virginia.

If the alias he then chose was a bit unimaginative, it was enough to conceal his true identity. If the stars had fixed his course far from home, the sea still beckoned him. And he answered its call.

Captain Paul grew to love his adopted country, and he would serve it well in the only way he knew how.

To one friend he entrusted the secret of his youth. It was in a letter . . . to Benjamin Franklin.

And now we know that the young ship's master who fought and ran away, had "not yet begun to fight."

All the while, he was identified by an alias . . . a name that was not his own, a name behind which he hid his past while he fought for us.

For it was he who lived to be the greatest naval captain of the American Revolution . . . under the assumed name of John Paul Jones.

18. DAUGHTER OF REBELLION

There is no greatest-ever movie. But if there were, it would have to be *Gone with the Wind*.

That's one of two reasons that every dainty debutante in Dixie wanted that starring role . . . including Catherine Campbell. Never before or since has there been such an expansive, expensive effort to cast a motion picture as for this American classic of the 1930s.

Leslie Howard balked at playing the challenging role of Ashley Wilkes. Even Clark Gable thought the part of Rhett Butler "too big an order."

Yet, in this biggest of the thespian big leagues, a fledgling actress . . . Atlanta-born Catherine Campbell . . . imagined herself worthy of the leading role . . . the symbol of deathless southern resistance . . . Scarlett O'Hara. That was the second reason.

For Scarlett O'Hara was to southern America what Joan of Arc had been to France . . . what Lady Godiva had been to England . . . what Mata Hari had been to Germany.

Scarlett O'Hara was the ultimate rebel. It must be remembered that women were barely emerging from their petticoat cocoon in the thirties.

Southern women still wore the scars of an un-Civil War that had rudely separated them from the genteel life of their mothers and had left them yet unemancipated. Here was a first big chance for a southern belle to win the war that their men had lost.

Catherine Campbell did not get the role of Scarlett O'Hara. Without her artistic talents, whatever they were, *Gone with the Wind* is still going.

Vivian Leigh got the role of Scarlett.

Clark Gable, because he needed money to pay off a divorce, became a superlative Rhett Butler. Who will ever forget his climactic curtain line?

Leslie Howard acquiesced to playing a part half his age, only when promised the co-production of another Selznick film.

Today, almost forty years later, *Gone with the Wind* is again playing first-run theaters! There is no comparable track record in the history of the motion-picture industry.

For a quarter century, *Gone with the Wind* was the biggest, and the most profitable.

If *Sound of Music, The Godfather, Jaws* took in more box-office dollars, they were by then cheaper dollars.

Yet, for all these superlative statistics, it was the social significance that made this movie monumental . . . the South did rise again!

No wonder Catherine Campbell wanted to be Scarlett O'Hara. Generations of moviegoers have walked the burning streets of Atlanta with her.

It was a world transfigured from plushly upholstered lives to guns and flames and reckless bravery and hopeless idealism. Yesterday's slaves became comrades in arms.

Scarlett O'Hara was a woman against the storm . . . bendable but unbreakable.

With Atlanta on fire she would not surrender: there's always tomorrow.

With Atlanta in ashes, Scarlett O'Hara would build anew: there's always tomorrow.

With her love gone, her life would go on.

As long as there is a Scarlett O'Hara, there will always be a tomorrow.

No; Catherine Campbell, the lovely lady of the Georgia gentry, did not get the part.

Perhaps she was "too delicate," "too fragile" to personify the Scarlett rebel.

But if her movie career ended before it began, her dream did not.

Indeed it came to life a generation later as a diabolically distorted nightmare.

For Catherine Campbell was to marry a San Francisco publisher . . . William Randolph Hearst.

You know their daughter . . . Patricia.

19. THE NAME OF THE GAME

I have a curious piece of history to relate to you; let's see if you can guess what I'm talking about.

During the quarter century between A.D. 1016 and 1042 England was occupied by the Danes . . . that is, Denmark had successfully invaded and taken over England.

I'd guess they were pretty rough about it, too, because hatred for the Danes lingered for quite some while after they were finally driven out of England.

Anyway, now the Danes are gone and this Englishman . . . we don't know his name . . . but this Englishman was digging around in one of the old battlefields when he unearthed a skull! The skull of some long-dead Danish soldier.

The Englishman was old enough to remember the days of Danish occupation, and this Hamlet-like experience of reminiscing over a skull just brought it all back to him . . . and was he angry!

He threw that skull on the ground and kicked it as hard as he could . . . and it felt good! So he kicked it again! And again, and again.

That's when some passers-by saw him kicking a skull around the pasture. When he explained what he was doing and how good it made him feel, they agreed that the Danes had been pretty rotten to the English. So they joined him!

Of course shoe toes weren't all that sturdy back then. When the new game of Danish Skull Kicking finally caught on throughout the countryside, there were a lot of sore feet. That's when someone got the idea of inflating a cow's bladder.

You know now what I'm about to say.

That day when a group of Englishmen got together and kicked a skull around a pasture . . . the first game of football was played.

Strange as its beginnings are, it's the *name* of the game that's most incongruous!

You'll agree why, after THE REST OF THE STORY.

As we all know, the modern game of football evolved from soccer and rugby. Those in turn came from kicking Danish skulls. Like baseball, then, football has its earliest roots in England.

But it's the "kicking" part I'd like to focus your attention on.

The early games were *kicking* games, and this hands-off restriction was not lifted until considerably late in the evolutionary pattern.

We're going to go back to England now . . . back to 1823 . . . to Rugby School. The famous Rugby School, where the game of rugby was innovated.

At any rate, Rugby was playing another school that day . . . they were down on the scoreboard . . . and desperate.

The rule was that all games end promptly at the stroke of five; they had a five o'clock bell, in fact. And the opponents, that day, kicked to Rugby just as the first stroke of five sounded! It was the last play of the game.

The ball was received by a player on the Rugby team named William Ellis. This chap was so frustrated at the thought of losing that he . . . well, he did something he shouldn't have.

What he should have done was to heel the ball and take a free kick, but instead he grabbed the ball, tucked it under his arm, ran for the goal, and scored just at the last stroke of the bell!

That was highly irregular and illegal, and Bill Ellis was in a whole lot of trouble.

His act of hanging onto the ball and running with it was decried as unfair, improper, unbecoming a gentleman, and a shocking violation of established order.

Nevertheless, it got people to thinking. Maybe it wasn't such a bad idea after all, taking the ball in your hands and running with it!

And of course, you know what happened after that. That one-time indiscretion became the innovation that's still with us today.

When you think of it, it's rather amusing . . . rather incongruous . . . that they'd been kicking the ball around for eight hundred years, and then the first time someone got his *hands* on it . . . it became what we now know as *football!*

20. FUTILITY

Best-selling books, big box office, and bombshell television specials are hitting us over the head with a new club.

Fact.

The once-popular strictly fiction format is gradually yielding to history, phasing out in favor of truth.

Example: *Roots*. ABC's twelve-hour, sure-fire winner. It held you . . . because it happened.

Here's another novel of historical significance: *Futility*. That's the name of the book, *Futility*, and you say you've not heard of it?

You'll wonder why you haven't, when I tell you THE REST OF THE STORY.

The novel *Futility* is about the maiden voyage of a fabulous ocean liner, a ship far larger than any previously built, labeled "unsinkable."

The vessel sets sail for New York from Southampton with a cargo of complacent passengers, strikes an iceberg en route, goes down.

And the ship was called . . . the *Titan*.

So why didn't author Morgan Robertson come right out and say it? His *Titan* . . . is obviously the *Titanic*.

Both liners were touted as the biggest, the grandest, the most luxurious . . . *and* foolproof.

Both struck icebergs on their maiden voyages between Southampton and New York.

Both were inadequately stocked with lifeboats, resulting in heavy casualties. And both sank at exactly the same spot in the North Atlantic, each on a cold April night.

It would seem clear that the real-life ship *Titanic* is the setting for the novel *Futility*, so why would the author have allowed for such minor discrepancies as these?

The *Titanic*, the *real* liner, displaced sixty-six thousand tons. Robertson's vessel, the *Titan*, displaced seventy thousand tons.

The *Titanic* was eight hundred eighty-two and one half feet long; Robertson rounded off *his* ship to eight hundred feet in length.

Even the apparent abbreviation of the name *Titanic* to *Titan* seems hardly worth the use of literary license.

After all, both liners were triple-screw, could travel up to twenty-five knots, could carry up to three thousand people.

All of the specific similarities were there, and yet author Morgan Robertson did not call it history.

Why?

In the first place, Robertson's characters, the passengers aboard the *Titan*, were purely fictional. Their personal interactions, problems, fears, were examined closely, and at last the ship sank. Hence the novel's title, *Futility*.

But there was another type of "futility" demonstrated in Robertson's book . . . a hopelessness that not even the author himself could have recognized.

For the novel that so accurately described an authentic disaster in the Atlantic, the book that charted an invisible course through the water to an appointment with death . . . owned up to its title beyond the wildest dreams of its readers.

For the literature that in every way seemed to recount . . . in reality *foretold*.

In 1898.

Fourteen years before the real-life *Titanic* set sail!

21. STRONG MAN'S WEAKNESS

Of all the torpedoes damned and Alamos remembered and fights not yet begun, one battle cry stands out among the rest. Simple, though it focuses on a complex man . . . strangely unwarlike, though it refers to one of history's most warlike warriors. . . .

"Let George do it!"

General George Smith Patton, Jr. . . . Old Blood and Guts . . . Georgie. Every imaginable nickname, both fond and ferocious, for the fabulous soldier some say was the last cavalier.

Athlete, poet, fatalist, mystic, historian, devout religionist, and consummate fighter . . . George Patton was a kaleidoscope of conflict, reflecting flakes of iron. But out of the discord there fused a harmony, a hurricane that swept Sicily and engulfed Europe and etched its way into the great battlefield of time.

It often seems that in the life of every great man a personal adversary must be contended with, a weakness must be turned to strength. So it was for George Patton. A somewhat sickly boy, he demanded of himself the courage and discipline that would mold him into an Olympic contestant at the age of twenty-six.

But there was another weakness in George's childhood . . . an enemy he never quite overcame. But that's THE REST OF THE STORY.

George Smith Patton, Senior. Lawyer. Son of a Civil War general. He never intended the life of a soldier for his son.

In spite of that, young George's heroes were clearly fixed in his mind. Alexander. Scipio. Cromwell. His idols were physically strong, so he made himself strong. They were brave, so he became brave. Their images forged his character, transfigured him into the soldier who would one day lead others through a hail of machine-gun fire. As a young lieutenant during World War I, George walked forward against a woods bristling with machine guns and, felled by a leaden burst that nearly tore off his left leg, clung to his consciousness and continued to direct his troops until relieved.

His sense of history gave him the will to do, or to die in the attempt. So completely did George Patton identify with those who had gone before him in war that he made a fetish of their courage, their accomplishments, and made theirs his.

A rugged, rawboned six-footer at Pasadena High School, he was handed a diploma and told to "go bowl them over at West Point." And bowl them over he did. Through West Point. Through two world wars. And through it all, the ghosts of warriors long dead haunted him, drove him on.

How curious the source of that earliest inspiration for a boy whose father encouraged the pursuit of law. There was another, an ally who fought beside George in his first childhood battles, who cheered him on as he acted out the game of war, whose robust nature, athletic ability, and equestrian talent helped to shape one of the greatest cavalrymen of all time.

That comrade of George's youth, who related the stories of Alexander and Scipio and Cromwell . . . had to. For George's very first enemies were the word, the sentence, the paragraph. And if he never completely conquered them, there was a reason for it. Until he was twelve, George Patton . . . could neither read nor write.

That was the strong man's weakness.

But the ally, the constant companion who read to him what he could not read . . . who first taught our nation's greatest cavalryman how to ride . . .

The friend of his youth who recognized the first beginnings of greatness in a small boy—and prepared him for a world of men—was a woman.

Mrs. George Patton, Senior. His mother.

22. THE LETTER

Edwin Thomas had a genuine genius for Shakespearean tragedy, so the drama critics have said for over a century. With whom might we compare him today. Olivier? Burton? Williamson?

During the latter half of the 1800s, in the midst of a legion of theatrical challengers, Edwin Thomas had few rivals. Although he was a wholly competent and versatile actor, this small, slight, dark man with the magnificent voice possessed an uncanny genius for tragedy. How ironic that his own life should have been so marked by it and that his fame should have been overshadowed, his spirit broken, and his reputation nearly ruined by an occurrence with which he had nothing to do!

He died with a letter in his pocket that might have set the record straight. But that's THE REST OF THE STORY.

Edwin Thomas made his acting debut at the age of fifteen, when he played Tressel to his father's Richard III. Two years later in New York, Edwin himself took the role of Richard III, but he was not to achieve any real acclaim until after his father's death, in 1852. In the years that followed, he met with phenomenal world-wide success. In New York he performed *Hamlet* for one hundred consecutive nights . . . in Boston he quickly overcame his contemporaries . . . in London he used the true text of Shakespeare, anticipating by years a similar reform in England.

Edwin had two brothers, John and Junius, who were also actors. Neither was of Edwin's stature, though the three together gave a memorable performance of *Julius Caesar* at New York's Winter Garden Theater in 1863. The fact that Edwin's brother, John, took the role of Brutus during that performance is particularly significant when you understand that he was on the brink of organizing a dark conspiracy in real life. Within two years, John would quietly enter the rear of a box in a Washington theater . . . and discharge a pistol at the head of President Abraham Lincoln. You see, Edwin Thomas' last name was Booth. His less gifted brother, in whom the assassin Brutus was reborn . . . was John Wilkes Booth.

There were two murders on that April night in 1865. The same gunshot that sent a ball deep into Abraham Lincoln's brain somehow sent another into the heart of Edwin Thomas Booth. The great actor's reputation eventually survived his brother's infamy, but his name, Edwin's, was to be obscured by the stigma of John's deed.

Shortly after the assassination, a disconsolate Edwin retired from the stage to agonize over the question "Why?" When he returned to the stage many years later, the bombast that characterized his earlier style was gone. Some critics say that the quieter, more introspective manner that replaced it singularly foreshadowed the realism of twentieth-century acting, but Edwin might have told them differently. He carried with him to his dying day one supreme, secret irony that at last made him one with the tragic characters to whom he confined himself. For Hamlet, Macbeth, and Othello the strutting was over, the fretting had begun . . . and a letter made the difference.

It was a letter of thanks for an act of courage at the peak of Edwin Booth's career. The actor was waiting on the station platform in Jersey City to board a train one evening when suddenly, without warning, the coach he was about to enter started with a jolt. Edwin turned fast, then broke into a cold sweat. A well-dressed young man nearby, pressed by the crowd, had lost his footing and fallen between the station platform and the moving train. Alert, Edwin locked one leg around a railing and, holding on with one hand, grabbed the boy by the collar with the other and pulled him back to safety. After sighs of relief were exchanged, the lad recognized his rescuer as the famous Edwin Booth. He shook the actor's hand warmly . . . expressed his gratitude. Edwin smiled and turned away.

Edwin did not recognize the admirer whom he had saved. He found out several weeks later in a letter from General Adam Badeau, Chief Secretary to General Ulysses S. Grant. He carried that bittersweet letter to his grave.

It was as though by some terrible tipping of the scales that Edwin had spared the son of his brother's victim. While one brother had killed the President, the other had saved the life of the President's son . . . Robert Todd Lincoln.

23. THE BULLY AND THE BOY

Bavaria. 1934.

It was the wrong time and the wrong place to be a Jew.

And Heinz was a Jew.

The little Bavarian village of Fürth was already overrun with Hitler's young thugs. To be a Jew . . . of any age . . . was to be a target.

And Heinz was only eleven.

It was the first minute of a black hour in European history. Some fled before the clock ran out. For many, time stood forever still. But Heinz was one of the lucky ones. And he would take with him . . . from that place of creeping horror . . . an indelible lesson with which one day he would make the whole world less dark.

Tradition, the song goes.

Heinz's father was a schoolteacher as had been his father before him.

Tradition.

The precepts of Judaism were carefully handed down from one generation to the next . . . and Heinz learned them well. The observance of the Sabbath, of Rosh Hashanah, of Yom Kippur.

But, for Heinz's parents, those ancient traditions had gained a new importance. They were a means of teaching their children self-control at a time when sudden impulse could be dangerous.

In the beginning, it was different.

Heinz started out in a cozy, close-knit little world. He vastly preferred soccer to school. A happy, often mischievous child, there were always tricks to play . . . pigtails to pull.

He was an undistinguished student, expounding at great length and with great flourish only when he knew the answers. But Heinz didn't always know the answers.

Then that black hour descended, as it always does . . . one second at a time.

Heinz's father was dismissed from his teaching post.

There were fewer and fewer soccer games.

Heinz was expelled, forced to attend an all-Jewish school.

Slowly the playful, exuberant boy became more cautious.

Slowly the streets became a battleground.

Hitler Youth roamed everywhere . . . but Heinz remembered what he'd been taught. There was no such thing as a sudden impulse. When a gang of bullies approached him on the street, he'd cross to the other side . . . when he could. Sometimes a beating was unavoidable. Sometimes it was not. Whatever the case, he must not pick a fight . . . and he must not speak up.

One day, the silence was broken . . . one day in 1934.

Eleven-year-old Heinz was forced into one of those inevitable confrontations with a Hitler bully, but this time . . . for the first time . . . he started talking. Perhaps it was about anything and everything. And perhaps Heinz himself didn't remember how he talked his way out of it . . . but he did talk his way out of it. And that was important.

Today, Heinz recalls his childhood in Bavaria.

"I was not acutely aware of what was going on. For children, these things are not serious . . . the political persecutions of my childhood are not what control my life. That part of my childhood was not a key to anything."

Maybe.

Or maybe the boy who talked his way out of a beating learned something that would one day be valuable to all of us.

Gratefully, Heinz and his family escaped Bavaria in time, made their way to America. Even there, he would cross the street whenever a group of boys walked his way. He'd been preconditioned to expect violence, I suppose.

But he never forgot how to talk . . . and if indeed the pen is mightier than the sword, for Heinz the spoken word is most powerful of all.

You see, he Americanized that Bavarian name when he arrived in New York.

And Heinz, who had negotiated that first peace settlement for himself . . . ultimately devoted his life toward a more peaceful world.

Henry Alfred . . . Kissinger.

History records that there was never a governor of New York so universally detested . . . as Lord Cornbury.

He was among New York's first governors. A colonial official.

One cannot help assuming that Lord Cornbury's hobby was largely responsible for his negative image. Oh, he was a rotten governor, all right. But it was his hobby, really, that made people distrust him. And Lord Cornbury's favorite pastime . . . is THE REST OF THE STORY.

Lord Cornbury was born in England in 1661, the eldest son of the second earl of Clarendon.

He served in Parliament for some sixteen years, after which he was appointed governor of New York and New Jersey.

Pursued by a long list of creditors, he eagerly accepted the opportunity to flee England, and at the age of forty Lord Cornbury arrived in the colonies.

The governors who had preceded him were nothing to brag about. But by the time Lord Cornbury was out of office, it was generally agreed that . . . well, let's put it this way: a colonial bumper sticker might have read "ABC: Anyone But Cornbury!"

It must have been the governor's hobby that caused the sentiment. He had a hobby that folks at that time found just plain disagreeable.

Now, again, I don't mean this to sound as though he was blameless in every other respect. Quite the opposite, in fact. Lord Cornbury was arrogant, despotic, grasping, dishonest. And he didn't even need to be! An account of two thousand pounds sterling was given him by the province assembly for transportation expenses. He didn't need that much.

His public-service salary was awarded him seven years in advance. He could hardly have used up all that money.

Or could he?

For Lord Cornbury had a hobby, an expensive one, and because he was an officially appointed governor, no one could do a thing about it.

As governor, he meddled in church politics quite a bit. Lord Cornbury rather favored the Church of England, so he made it uncomfortable for New York's prevalent Presbyterians. He even had a couple of Presbyterian ministers thrown in the slammer . . . illegally, of course. Supposedly they'd been preaching without a license, and it took nothing less than an Episcopalian jury to get them off the hook.

And when Lord Cornbury was not feeding Presbyterians to Episcopalians, he was petitioning the New York legislature for more money. When they resisted, he dissolved their assembly.

Then he tried New Jersey.

And they resisted.

And he pulled the same stunt with them.

Now there was nothing left but to misappropriate funds, funds that should have gone to the fortification of the seacoast and to other important purposes. Instead, they went to the support of Lord Cornbury's hobby. The people were dumbstruck.

Finally, Queen Anne got wind of what was going on. In 1708, she bounced the six-year governor of New York and New Jersey and put Lord Lovelace in Lord Cornbury's place.

I guess you could say that Lord Cornbury got what was coming to him. No sooner was he out of office than his creditors nabbed him. After a spell in debtors' prison, he returned to England and entered the House of Lords as the third earl of Clarendon.

As far as we know, he took his expensive hobby with him. Lord Cornbury . . . loved clothes. He collected costly clothing.

I mean, while he was governor of New York and New Jersey, he just had to be the snappiest dresser in the colonies.

It was a lifelong hobby of his. For from the time he was eight years old until he died, at sixty-two, every day . . . day and night . . . Lord Cornbury . . . dressed like a woman.

25. THE RELUCTANT VAMPIRE

Actor George Reeves put a gun to his head . . . pulled the trigger. Now he's dead.

But the bullet couldn't have been lead . . . perhaps it was Kryptonite.

You see, George Reeves was Superman . . . really *was* Superman to millions of TV viewers and for what must have seemed like millions of years . . . to George.

If he'd merely acted the part . . . if George had been an actor who'd taken the role for a day or the run of a play . . . perhaps the sad story of Superman would have ended differently.

Instead, the Man of Steel scrawled a trembling farewell, explaining that there was no work for him outside that fabled phone booth. Then he took a revolver and vanquished the hero no villain could vanquish.

But the question remains: Did George jump the gun? Was he too quick on the trigger during a solitary hour of melancholy?

It's true that his typecast popularity precluded a preponderance of diverse roles.

This isn't meant to demean, but if George had been a truly versatile actor, wouldn't his day have come? Would the world have been forced to forget the comic-book character from Krypton?

We won't seek to answer that question here. But there's another story about another actor that might help you decide.

His name was DeForest.

DeForest was born into posh New York society almost eighty years ago. His father declared that his son would go to Yale, but failing grades and misconduct prevented that dream.

Once expelled from school, eighteen-year-old DeForest joined the Navy . . . but it didn't change his luck. Smashed in the mouth and badly injured by an escaping prisoner, three days solitary on bread and water for an "accidental" AWOL, he turned to the civilian job market as all that was left.

But that didn't work out either. He was no good at the National Biscuit Company. He was no good as a tugboat inspector. Eventually, he stumbled into the job he would keep for the rest of his life. Acting.

And DeForest was a good actor . . . perhaps even a great one. That's what made the difference. A decade would bring him to Hollywood, then through another decade, a string of uneven movie roles.

One such role was in a picture called *The Return of Dr. X*, a vampire movie. And DeForest made a terribly convincing vampire! Audiences cringed at the hollow eyes, the sallow complexion, the bared fangs. Perhaps at last DeForest had found his niche in life. After all, he was perfect for the part. And some movie makers had given up on him as a strong lead, because that injury dealt him by an escaping prisoner during his Navy years had left him with a speech impediment.

A less gifted actor would have stopped there . . . as a vampire. For DeForest, it was only the beginning.

He took those ten years of fractured movie roles and turned them into triumph. The next seventeen years, which might have been spent as a reluctant vampire . . . bore his own authentic stamp instead.

For the lisp from a smashed lip had by then become a trademark.

A lesser thespian might have been nailed by a typecast stake of holly . . . but this creature of *All Through the Night* flew the crypt.

He traded the bat for *The Maltese Falcon*.

And while others played out . . . he played it again. . . .

Humphrey DeForest . . . Bogart.

26. A TRUTH OF GRAIN

The sacking of agricultural officials has become a virtual tradition in the Soviet Union. A recent Kremlin house cleaning swept agricultural minister Dimitri Polyansky and his two deputies right out of office.

And they won't be the last.

In fact, it's so hard to make Russian soil grow grain that Professor R. B. Farrell of Northwestern University calls the Soviet Union's agricultural ministry "one of the most dangerous assignments in the country."

Of course, bounced bigwigs are merely targets for a scapegoat-seeking Kremlin. Even Khrushchev's fall was partly due to an ineffective farm policy.

There's been a lot of guessing as to why Soviet grain yields are so predictably pitiful each year—bad weather, bad resources, and so forth—but the basic truth of the matter is that the Russians just can't seem to grow the stuff!

Few remember the golden-egg-laying goose they booted out of the nest, but that's THE REST OF THE STORY.

For all the flavors of religious diversity in the United States, the Mennonites leave a particularly pleasant taste on the public's palate.

Theirs is a warm, quiet breed that believes in neither oaths nor infant baptism nor military service nor the acceptance of public office. They favor inobtrusive dress and plain living, and in their own very special way, they're remarkably colorful.

The Mennonites. We owe them.

During the 1890s, the Atchison, Topeka and Santa Fe was selling large tracts of land in Kansas. What they really wanted was homesteaders to farm this land and send their crops to market by rail. The Mennonites were among the first takers.

Now, when these Mennonites moved to Kansas, they perpetuated their gentle traditions . . . continued their unassuming lives . . . grew wheat in their own special way from their own special seed.

Then came the big drought. The worst in years. It was so bad that the Department of Agriculture sent an expert from Washington to examine the withered crops. And it must have been a barren sight . . . acre upon acre of parched Kansas prairie.

Then the government inspector came to the Mennonites' land. What he found started a revolution on the plains. While others' wheat had failed . . . had been starved and blistered by the drought . . . the Mennonites' wheat was thriving, reaching bravely for the killer sun!

In Kansas today, the Mennonite strain of wheat seed is still being used. So hearty is this strain that it can be planted in the fall and harvested in the spring, actually resisting "winter kill." Needless to say, drought continues to be a small obstacle for Mennonite wheat to overcome.

Now let me direct your attention to some 1975 Soviet statistics: The Russians needed to harvest a hundred and eighty-five million tons of grain to meet domestic demands. Because of a formidable drought, they got only a hundred and forty million. To avoid mass starvation, the Soviets bought wheat . . . from the United States.

Wouldn't Russia be lucky to have the Mennonites! Well, at one time . . . they did.

Nearly a century ago, there were Mennonites in Russia. But remember, their religion precludes the taking up of arms . . . and that's just what the Czar wanted them to do. With Europe periodically in turmoil, people who would not go to war for their ruler were particularly unwelcome. That included the Mennonites. At any rate, they were kicked out, and guess where they came. . . .

That's right. The same Mennonites who were forced to leave Russia came to America . . . where religious freedom was a written promise. Where they would not be forced to compromise their ideals, their way of life.

And you might be interested to know that they were invited to the United States by the Atchison, Topeka and Santa Fe . . . by railroad agents who were selling land in Kansas. It was a matter of coincidence that the Mennonites brought with them wheat seeds . . . called "red wheat" . . . from their homeland in the Crimea.

What the story boils down to is this: If the Mennonites had not been driven out of Russia . . . the United States, instead of selling, might now be buying wheat . . . from the Russians.

27. HELLO, SUCKER!

Meet Mary Louise.

She was born in Waco, Texas, in 1884. Her father was a wholesale grocer, both parents Irish immigrants.

By the age of fourteen, talented Mary Louise began studying voice in Chicago and subsequently became a traveling performer.

City to city.

Stage companies, rodeos.

In 1904, she met and married a Denver newspaperman.

The marriage would not last. Nor would her second. . . . Nor would her third. . . .

For little Mary Louise had her eye on New York and the big time. Soon she became the woman you know . . . the bright, tough roustabout of night club stage and silent screen . . . Mary Louise Cecilia . . . "Texas" Guinan.

Once on stage in New York City, Mary Guinan rose quickly from the ranks of the chorus. One good musical comedy role followed by another, better one.

By 1908 Mary was on the vaudeville circuit, billed as "The Gibson Girl." There, she belted ballads from a basket suspended above the audience.

The year 1913 brought a successful revue, *The Passing Show*.

World War I took Mary behind the lines in France, to entertain the troops.

It was perhaps in silent films that Mary first hammered out the image of "Texas" Guinan. Such pictures as *The Gun Woman* and *Little Miss Deputy*. For the aggressive self-reliance Mary dramatized on screen forged the character of a new woman . . . brash, capable, ready and willing to meet the male world on its own terms.

That was the role "Texas" Guinan carried into the night clubs and the lounges, the speakeasies of the Prohibition Era.

She became the lusty performer-hostess, a white-hot neon doll glowing through a stale haze of cigar smoke . . . a husky, dusky reflection in a pool of illegal booze.

"Texas" Guinan. Her trade, trading insults. Her greeting, "Hello, sucker!"

The El Fay Club opened in 1924, "Texas" Guinan perched atop a tall stool, jibing with the socialites and the racketeers. They were her court, her reign, her throne, her subjects.

The El Fay, raided, closed. The *Del* Fay opened two blocks away.

The Texas Guinan Club, the 300 Club, the Club Intime, Texas Guinan's Salon Royal. Each in succession. An itinerant kingdom, uprooted at the shriek of a police whistle.

"Give the little girl a great big hand!"

And they gave her a hand.

But newsman Lowell Thomas remembers another "Texas" Guinan from many years before, a young woman named Mary.

That's right. In Anaconda, Montana, when Thomas was twelve, he had a crush on a vivacious blonde named Mary Guinan.

Lowell never told his folks about the infatuation . . . but as the years rolled by, he watched that gleaming star from his childhood ascend and take its place in the midnight sky.

For the little girl from Waco who rode the road shows to New York City . . . the brash blonde who bombarded the Big Apple, belting ballads from a swinging basket . . . the speakeasy mistress of ceremonies who blazed a brazen trail across the Prohibition Era . . . "Texas" Guinan . . . Lowell Thomas remembers as his . . . school teacher. His *Sunday* school teacher!

And now you know THE REST OF THE STORY.

28. MADNESS IN THE AIR

Two couples went out for the evening, in much the same way couples everywhere do.

There was dinner . . . and a show . . . and there was madness in the air.

One couple was married. The other, engaged. And while the marriage of the first was not without turmoil, the union of the second was most promising indeed . . . until madness struck.

It's been suggested that when the insane were locked away, in days gone by, it was because the so-called sane feared the contagion of insanity. In other words, many believed madness to be "catching" . . . like a disease. In an effort to immunize themselves, they packed off the "crazies" to faraway places, believing they might avoid thereby the afflictions of the mad.

Of course, this isolation of the insane . . . was insane. And while there are some communicable diseases that manifest unusual behavior in the victim . . . and while we have traced some forms of insanity, such as schizophrenia, to blood disorders and vitamin deficiencies . . . there is no modern-day evidence that madness, as such, can be caught like a cold.

Almost no evidence.

For occasionally the precepts of medieval medicine . . . and Dark Ages psychiatry . . . come back to haunt us.

Once upon a time, two couples went out for the evening . . . in much the same way couples everywhere do. And there is a REST OF THE STORY.

There was dinner . . . and a show . . . and perhaps even madness in the air. How else could what happened to them have happened to them?

Let's take the four, one at a time.

A distant relative of actor Basil Rathbone.

Major Henry Rathbone. Intelligent, honest . . . a good army officer. As far as we know, any predisposition to violence he might have had began and ended with the military.

Major Henry's companion for the evening was his fiancée, Clara Harris. An attractive, gentle woman, she one day married the major . . . despite what happened that night.

Third in the party was Mary. High-spirited, quick-witted, well educated, Mary came from a rather distinguished family. Some of her relatives frowned on the man she had married, who accompanied her that evening. And even he, from time to time, doubted that any man could make Mary happy. Nevertheless, they'd been engaged, broken it off, become engaged again . . . and finally married.

They had four children, only one of whom survived to adulthood. And though Mary and her husband seemed truly to love each other, their marriage was often beset by hectic quarrels and perhaps-unfounded jealousies.

Then, one day, the scales, already precariously balanced, began to tip. Mary started to suffer from recurring headaches, fits of temper, and a sense of insecurity and loneliness that was intensified by her husband's long absences on the lawyer's circuit.

Although this is not meant to suggest that the creeping madness that began that night began with Mary, she was later adjudged, certified, insane.

For, once upon a time, two couples went out together. There must have been madness in the air.

Major Henry eventually married Clara . . . and shortly thereafter, in a fit of inexplicable rage, murdered her.

And on the very evening the four shared each other's company, Mary's husband was killed in cold blood . . . by a man decidedly insane. And that man, days later, was gunned down by another . . . who also went mad.

If the chain remains unbroken, what you've heard is all we know.

And if there was madness in the air that night, perhaps it lingers still.

For two couples went out together that night in Washington, D.C., . . . in 1865. There was dinner . . . and a show . . . at Ford's Theater.

29. THE GOOD-FOR-NOTHING

When you're a little boy and Dad calls you "good-for-nothing," it's just got to hurt!

That's just what Guiseppe's Papa called him . . . good-for-nothing. Little Guiseppe good-for-nothing.

And he wasn't joking!

For Papa came from a family of fishermen. Three hundred years the men in his family had been fishermen in Sicily. And Papa himself was a fisherman.

When he first came to America, he worked on the railroad until he'd saved enough money to send for his wife. Then he headed straight for San Francisco, to Fisherman's Wharf . . . to become a fisherman again . . . to perpetuate the family tradition.

Eventually, Papa and Mama had nine children. And you can imagine that all of the boys got their sea legs early . . . began helping Papa out on his fishing boat from the time they learned to walk.

All of them, that is, except Guiseppe.

Guiseppe didn't want to.

"What do you mean, you don't want to!" demanded Papa.

Guiseppe explained that the rocking of the small boat and the smell of the fish made him ill. It wasn't that he didn't want to help out; fish just didn't agree with him, that's all.

That wasn't good enough for Papa. As far as Papa was concerned, Guiseppe was good for nothing. The boy had come from a long line of fishermen and there was no reason in the world for the profession to disagree with him. Guiseppe was never too sick to go out and play with his friends. Why, then, did it make him sick to help his Papa?

Not why but what happened then is THE REST OF THE STORY.

Disturbed by his father's criticism, young Guiseppe tried very hard to adapt to the family business. The rocking of the boat and the smell of the fish still bothered him, so he turned to other tasks, such as sealing the boat and repairing the nets. But as hard as he'd try to remain unaffected, the fish smell was still in the gear and made his already sensitive stomach even more queasy.

Guiseppe quit.

He went out and odd-jobbed wherever he could. Errand boy. Newspaper boy. Sometimes he even pulled down a dollar a day. It wasn't pocket money; it was table money. Every cent Guiseppe earned, he turned over to the household for food and clothing.

You'd think Papa would be proud of his son, but to Papa young Guiseppe was just being lazy. Odd jobs were lazy jobs, according to him. Real work was helping Papa on the fishing boat.

This weighed pretty heavily on the lad. He started hiding under the bed when Papa came looking for him. Or he ran off to play sports with his friends when he knew Papa was about to call him to the fishing boat.

Tennis was especially interesting to him, watching the older boys play. He knew that tennis champs Maurice McLaughlin and Bill Johnston came from San Francisco, and he wanted to be like them.

But the tennis passion didn't last long, and for the first time Guiseppe began to believe his Dad. Perhaps he was a lazy good-for-nothing who couldn't even stay interested in a sport. Maybe he never *would* amount to anything.

That's the way Guiseppe saw it back then. Everything just seemed sort of gloomy and hopeless.

But as it turned out, Guiseppe one day became the most successful member of his family!

Oh, he didn't go back to fishing. Despite his ancestry, Guiseppe just wasn't cut out to be a fisherman. Or a tennis player, for that matter.

When Guiseppe finally found something that interested him sufficiently to stay with it, his passion for it was so great that two of his brothers quit fishing and joined him!

You've heard of Guiseppe by his American first name. Everyone else has, I guess, and that great big world beyond Fisherman's Wharf won't forget the fisherman they lost.

Neither will they forget the boy who forgot about tennis only to enter the world of sports and turn it upside down.

For if that young man hadn't been too seasick to join the family business, he would have left a vacancy in baseball's Hall of Fame too great to fill. . . .

Guiseppe . . . Joe . . . DiMaggio.

30. GENERAL TAYLOR'S LAST BATTLE

For the military man, communication will always be supremely important. Just think of what it must have been like in the days of General Taylor. Only a handful of telegraph lines, and those to the major cities. The telephone and short-wave radio still many decades in the future.

The United States Postal Service was about all they had back then, and that institution nearly cost General Taylor his last and most important assignment to battle.

General Taylor was just plain cut out for army life.

His daddy was a colonel in the Revolutionary War . . . moved to Kentucky, then to a part of Virginia, in 1785. The colonel's only neighbors were fellow Revolutionary War veterans, and it was on his farm near the present city of Louisville that Colonel Taylor brought up his five boys to be soldiers. One became a general.

Three long wars went into the forging of this magnificent military superstrategist, the future General Taylor. A captain before the War of 1812, he was promoted to the rank of major during it. Finally, after ten years' service as lieutenant colonel and the myriad battles that constituted the Indian campaigns, he received the rank of brigadier general. In 1840, General Taylor was assigned to duty in Louisiana, where he acquired a house and a large, outlying plantation. But within six years, the general was ordered by the War Department to take up a position along the southern border of Texas. The Mexican War was just beginning.

For the next year, reports of General Taylor's brilliant victories made news across the nation. At last, in February of 1847, the sixty-two-year-old warrior led his troops over the mountains to Saltillo. The battle of Buena Vista, they called it. General Santa Anna's Mexican forces outnumbered the Americans four to one, but General Taylor outmaneuvered his adversary.

This victory made the old general a national hero. But when the Mexican War was over, he remembered his plantation near Baton Rouge and became eager to return to the country. With almost boyish delight, the general packed a few belongings and sped back to this solitary refuge from the many battles of his life. There, couched in crimson flowers and pleasant fields and magnolia trees, General Taylor sought for a while to forget about war.

But, for all his seclusion, there was still much mail . . . many letters of congratulations from friends and strangers . . . fan mail, you might say. Despite the general's gratitude at receiving it, an increasing amount of this correspondence posed quite a financial dilemma for the veteran of three wars.

"Insufficient postage," came the weekly announcement from General Taylor's local postmaster. "Insufficient postage on this one, and this one too . . . and here's another!"

The old warrior must have quietly mused over the irony. He had ignored that last communiqué from Washington during the Mexican War . . . had crossed the mountains to Saltillo anyway. If he'd guessed wrong on that one, he might have lost more than his command. Now the Mexican War was over, but his mail was still causing him problems.

We don't know exactly how much inadequately covered correspondence General Taylor accumulated during those months at Baton Rouge, but it must have been quite a lot. Enough at least to cause him to decline the acceptance of any more. So much, anyway, that his postmaster, having no more room for it, was eventually forced to send it all to the dead-letter office in Washington.

General Taylor's story might have ended here were it not for a friend who visited him several weeks later, resulting in THE REST OF THE STORY.

In the middle of salad and coffee one day, the old general's friend offhandedly remarked that a very important letter should have arrived from Philadelphia long ago. Why hadn't the general received it? His friend wanted to know.

"Received what?" asked General Taylor anxiously. "Another assignment?"

Well, in a manner of speaking it was.

Uncomfortable days passed until the dead letters were all returned from Washington. There, with all those unopened letters, was General Taylor's last call to battle, and he'd nearly missed it.

Having spent so many years in the upper echelon of the military, General Taylor was seldom called by his first name. Zachary. And though his hard-earned title of general was set aside during the last sixteen months of his life, it was replaced with an even more impressive one.

That "dead letter" was from a political convention in Philadelphia. General Taylor's last battle . . . was for the presidency of the United States.

For many, the process of research and development is all in the family . . . for the Curies, for Masters and Johnson. . . .

And so it was for Jakob and Wilhelm.

They were scholars . . . researchers.

Although they died while working on a thirty-two volume dictionary . . . a monument to their tireless scholarly efforts . . . it is another piece of research for which we remember them.

They were boys in college . . . Jakob and Wilhelm . . . when their interest in history was first aroused. In a way, you might say they were the first psychological anthropologists . . . the first to explore the relation of folklore to human history. They perused the writings of Homer . . . presumably fiction . . . discovered their impact and the possible links to fact. Perhaps, they decided, other legends might shed new light on the greater story of man . . . the true story.

Some such legends had been previously collected, published . . . but many others had never been written down. This was the elusive category called "oral tradition" . . . and only a few aged peasants, here and there, remembered them. When they died, the stories . . . some dating back a thousand years . . . would die with them.

So when Jakob was twenty-two and Wilhelm twenty-one, the

two set out to record these legends . . . to seek their tellers before they and their stories vanished forever.

These young men were scholars, remember . . . and their quest was one of historical relevance . . . so they were perhaps at first amazed by what they found in the beginnings of their research. But then the chore began to cheer them, with the passing of each day. The people they met proved most interesting indeed.

A shepherd was happy to spend an afternoon spinning old yarns for a bottle of wine . . . an old cavalry sergeant come upon hard times told a few more in return for a patched pair of pants.

One woman, living in a home for the aged, was hesitant to talk to them. If she were overheard telling her stories to anyone but children, they might lock her up for a madwoman, she said. So Wilhelm got a friend to take along his children as an audience for the old woman . . . while Wilhelm listened and took notes behind a curtain.

The best story source turned out to be a tailor's wife. Not only did she tell her stories well, but she told them each time in exactly the same words. If she spoke too quickly and was asked to repeat, she would retell them slowly, without a change.

After five hard but happy years, Jakob and Wilhelm had collected eighty-six stories. But at the last, they were unable to draw any particular historical significance from them.

So the manuscripts were shelved . . . and might still be there today, were it not for a friend who discovered them and insisted that they be published.

Arrangements were made with a printer in Berlin, and a few days before Christmas of 1812, the first edition of Jakob and Wilhelm's stories went on sale.

Expecting so little, they accepted no money at first, and at last took only a pittance.

At no time in their subsequent careers as librarians and professors did they have a year's income equivalent to more than five thousand dollars.

And yet their little book of stories would one day sell a billion copies in twenty thousand editions . . . would be translated into fifty languages in forty countries.

Today, a century and a half later, their little volume is second only to the Bible as most famous, most widely read, most generally remembered.

They were brothers, Jakob and Wilhelm.

Like George and Ira . . . Wilbur and Orville . . . they kept it all in the family.

But such was the magnitude of Jakob and Wilhelm's last name, that you only remember them by it.

And if the historical relevance of their first work together less than pleased them, their stories have since pleased a hundred and fifty years of children.

Stories like "Hansel and Gretel" . . . and "Snow White" . . . and "Cinderella" . . . and "Tom Thumb."

For the book they called *Tales for Children and The Hearth*, you know . . . as *Grimm's Fairy Tales*.

And now you know the brothers Grimm . . . and their REST OF THE STORY.

32. WHO WAS THAT MASKED MAN?

It was in many ways a very ordinary crime for the city of Chicago . . . and at that, a non-violent one. In one sense, the robbery that occurred during the night of Friday, June 18, 1976, was the most ironic you're likely to hear about for a while.

Sixty-one-year-old Clay had driven all the way from California in his Dodge van. He was here on business, he told police later, and very tired when he checked into the Hyatt House.

The van was parked in a lot outside his room . . . under a light, in fact . . . and Clay could see it from his window. But he was asleep that night . . . when the robbery took place.

Next morning, Clay got up, got dressed, and walked out to the parking lot to discover that his van had been ransacked. There were a tape recorder, a pair of binoculars, an outboard motor, and brand-new fishing gear . . . even a cache of ammunition. But all that was left behind, unharmed. All they'd stolen . . . was his gun.

When the investigating officer raised an eyebrow, Clay explained that it was an antique . . . an 1866 Remington revolver. And its possession was all right because he, Clay, was a lawman himself.

How strange that this particular lawman would one day meet his match in Chicago, outwitted by a petty crook!

"I'll remember to hook up my alarm system next time," he said.

And who might have guessed that this symbol of justice was to sleep through the only real crime he ever knew . . . and that someone else would have to avenge it for him?

"There will be retribution!" he assured everyone, with a barely perceptible smile.

And somebody was heard to say, as he mounted the Dodge van and drove on his way, "Who was that masked man?"

Why, he's Clayton Moore. The Lone Ranger.

33. COME OUT WITH MY HANDS UP!

A hundred and fifty years ago, India was a storybook country . . . a Kipling country before Kipling was born.

It was a land of extremes. Of diamonds and dirt. Tigers and elephants roamed free, and ancient customs could call for human sacrifice.

This was a time of bazaars and turbans and beads and barbarity. The air was teeming with more brutal exuberance than Times Square today.

This was the era of fire-eaters and maharajas who wore exquisite silks embroidered with gold and gems.

And it was during this time that the country was roamed by a robber gang, a strange and barbaric underground society known as the Thugs.

Aside from their raids on the rich, the Thugs killed in the name of their Hindu goddess, the goddess of destruction. But the blood of their victims could not be spilled, so their trademark was strangling.

One leader dared to oppose the Thugs. He was the rajah of Kolhapur.

India's rajah of Kolhapur came to his state's throne in 1822, by accident. His elder brother, who was first in line, had died. Perhaps because of it, because of the speed of his inheritance, the rajah felt even more responsibility toward Kolhapur's government . . . had an even greater desire to keep what he had.

Now, the rajah of Kolhapur was not exactly what you'd call a tyrant, but he was a law-and-order man. Back in the 1820s, his state was the only territory in the country not affected by British rule. The thought of British interference perturbed him so that he sent his own armies to neighboring states to help drive out the British.

But the rajah's real enemy . . . the real threat to his kingdom . . . was the Thugs, the organized band of terrorists and thieves. By night, they raided his treasury . . . murdered his subjects . . . laid waste the Kolhapur countryside. And the situation was worsening.

First the rajah tried to increase his personal army. He threw a ring of guards around his hoards of valuables and around himself. To no avail. The onslaught continued, more furiously than ever.

At last, one morning, the rajah awakened to find many of his favorite jewels stolen and their guard lying lifeless in a pool of blood. The rajah's dark eyes flashed in anger as he turned to his marshals.

"These devils must be stopped!" he demanded, his voice shaking with rage.

The marshals glanced at each other fearfully, until one attendant suggested that this pilferage and destruction might, in fact, *not* be the work of the Thugs! Usually, the Thugs worked by day, he said, and they were forbidden by their own perverse religion to spill blood.

The rajah looked down at his murdered guard. He had been mutilated. Repelled, the rajah looked away. "But who else could it be?" he said. His voice was quiet now, whispering, tense. His marshals were silent. "Whoever they are," said the rajah with renewed strength, "whoever they are, I want their leader caught, and I want him killed, and I want him now!"

But, you know, they never caught him.

So the rajah was to live out most of the rest of his life tormented by these villains. By night, they would ravage the state of Kolhapur, steal from the treasury, and terrorize the rajah's subjects. And they never caught the ringleader of this destructive

band for one, simple reason. The few who knew his identity . . .
while he lived . . . dared not tell.

You see, in the early-nineteenth century, the state of Kolhapur
had its own Jekyll and Hyde.

By day, the rajah was a proud and defending sovereign. By night,
he led a band of cutthroat robbers . . . and plundered his own
kingdom . . . and stole from himself. That is THE REST OF THE
STORY.

34. EXECUTION FIT FOR A KING

Where do you stand on capital punishment?

In modern times, you don't have much choice. You're either for or against.

Nearly two hundred years ago, if you'd committed a serious crime and were sentenced to death, how you died depended on who you were.

That was about the time the good Dr. Joseph came out of nowhere . . . and changed things for the better.

What this eighteenth-century humanitarian got for his trouble, is THE REST OF THE STORY.

Dr. Joseph was a humanitarian to some, a bleeding heart to others.

Deep down, I suspect he was against capital punishment, but he realized he'd get nowhere with that conviction. After all, we're talking about the 1700s.

So Dr. Joseph contented himself with a personal crusade against the accepted methods of execution. They were all unnecessarily cruel, he maintained. They were all, in some way, linked to torture.

Dr. Joseph had no real voice in the matter. He was just one doctor, and there were plenty of them.

In 1789, he managed to get himself elected to the constituent assembly. There, at least, he would have something to say about the laws concerning capital punishment.

Immediately after his election, Dr. Joseph began a campaign against cruelty. He was the assembly's token liberal, and he drew more than a little laughter from his distinguished, politically experienced colleagues.

It's all well and good to criticize, they said, but what was the alternative Dr. Joseph had in mind? How could there ever be such a thing as a humane execution?

That was a good question. For all his concern, he had failed to recommend a viable alternative.

Dr. Joseph kept his mouth shut. He began to research the history of execution. Looking for an answer, he delved into the ancient, forgotten books that described capital punishment through the ages. Then he perused the laws of other countries, their customs of dealing with crime. Somewhere there had to be a solution. At last Dr. Joseph discovered it.

Excited over what he found, the good doctor hurried to the next assembly meeting, bearing a folder bulging with the data he had studied.

It appeared that the Italians had already come up with the ideal means of doing away with a prisoner. They called it *mannaia*. It was an optional execution, for those of noble birth. You might say, an execution fit for a king.

Once again, the assemblymen shook their heads, though this time there was no laughter. For what Dr. Joseph had described to them was, in fact, among the very few absolutely effective, positively painless means of bringing death.

So the official word was released: The ancient form of execution *mannaia* was under scrutiny by the constituent assembly. Tests were performed on cadavers. Analyses were made. The results were satisfactory. A vote was taken. And on April 25, 1792, three hard-fought years after Dr. Joseph's campaign had begun, *mannaia* was put to use.

Dr. Joseph had won . . . almost.

No, Dr. Joseph was never to become a victim of his humane contraption. Remember, he was a gentle man, much respected and well-loved.

In fact, when Dr. Joseph's countrymen saw the sense of humanitarian execution . . . when they realized it was a step forward toward a more civil civilization . . . they honored the good doctor by naming it after him.

And that's how Dr. Joseph lost.

For the crude instrument he helped to refine . . . the machine from an Italian archive . . . rose from the pages of history to inspire terror forever after.

Oh, as means of death go, this noblemen's form of execution is still perhaps the most humane. The problem was, it did not appear to be.

Yet the *mannaia* got a new lease on death and another name from the man who, singlehandedly, had resurrected it.

But the gentle doctor's children, in time, changed their names . . . to avoid being associated with Dr. Joseph . . . Guillotin.

35. BAD, BAD ED O'HARE

The speckles in the Pacific night sky were bombers. Nine twin-engine Japanese bombers, in formation, on course to their target: the aircraft carrier *Lexington*.

Butch O'Hare could see them all clearly from the cockpit of his Grumman Wildcat F4F. He was their lone-wolf pursuer, tagging along in the darkness. If he did not seize the opportunity now to attack from the rear, his home base, the carrier *Lexington*, would be obliterated—sent to the ocean floor in fragments of twisted steel.

So Butch gripped the controls, palms sweating in anticipation of what he knew he must do. The engine roared and the Wildcat lunged for its prey.

Before it was over, five of the nine Japanese bombers had been dumped into the Pacific. Butch was ripping away at a sixth when he ran out of ammunition . . . and his comrades arrived to finish the job.

That was February 20, 1942, and the daring of Lieutenant Commander Edward Henry "Butch" O'Hare . . . the Navy's number-one World War II ace, the first naval aviator ever to win the Congressional Medal of Honor.

A year later, Butch went down in aerial combat. But his home towners would not allow the memory of that heroic accomplishment to die.

So the next time you fly into Chicago's O'Hare International Airport, you'll know for whom it was named, and why. What you don't yet know is that you'll be passing through a shrine . . . a monument to a very special kind of love . . . and that's THE REST OF THE STORY.

Chicago. The Roaring Twenties. The time and territory of gangster Al Capone.

And of all the Capone cronies . . . of all the unsavory soldiers who served in that army of crime . . . only one earned the nickname "Artful Eddie."

Eddie was the fast lawyer's fast lawyer. Through his loopholes walked the most glamorous rogues in the gallery of gangland.

In 1923, Eddie himself was indicted on an illegal booze deal, two hundred thousand dollars' worth, but he won his own reversal.

Later, Al Capone picked up Eddie and put him in charge of the dog tracks nationwide. You see, Eddie had already swiped the patent on the mechanical rabbit.

Pretty soon Artful Eddie, as the Capone syndicate representative, became known as the undisputed czar of illegal dog racing. Nothing could have been easier to rig in favor of the mob. Eight dogs running . . . overfeed seven . . . it was as simple as that. In no time, Artful Eddie became a wealthy man.

Then, one day, for no apparent reason, Eddie squealed on Capone. He wanted to go straight, he told the authorities. What did they want to know?

The authorities were understandably skeptical. Why should Artful Eddie, the pride of the underworld, seek to undermine his own carefully constructed dog-track empire? Didn't Eddie know what it meant . . . to rat on the mob?

He knew.

Then, what was the deal? What could he possibly hope to gain from aiding the government, that he didn't already have? Eddie had money. Eddie had power. Eddie had the pledged security of the one and only Al Capone. What was the hitch?

That's when Artful Eddie revealed the hitch. There was only one thing that really mattered to him. He'd spent his life among the disreputable and despicable. After all was said and done, there was only one who deserved a break.

His son.

So Eddie squealed . . . and the mob remembered . . . and in time, two shotgun blasts would silence him forever.

Eddie never lived to see his dream come true. But it did. For as he cleansed the family name of the underworld stain, his son became acceptable to . . . was accepted by . . . Annapolis. He became the flying ace who downed five bombers and went on to win the Congressional Medal of Honor.

So the next time you fly into Chicago's O'Hare International Airport, remember Butch O'Hare . . . and his daddy, Edward J. "Artful Eddie," the crook who one day went mysteriously straight . . . and paid with his own life for his son's chance to make good.

Once upon a time, in a land of leaden skies and creeping fogs and flat, barren countryside, there lived a boy. His name was Dietz Edzard. The place was Bremen, Germany.

In keeping with the Hanseatic tradition of his home town, Dietz entered the export trade. But even then, at sixteen, his heart was elsewhere.

Today we find it remarkable that such sensitivity was nurtured in the midst of stern and practical people. But it was that same sensitivity that made young Dietz long for a life of grace and elegance . . . and a career as an artist.

Eventually he would have both.

And so it was, in the sparkling mecca for artists everywhere, that Dietz Edzard came to paint a portrait some say is enchanted.

May 31, 1961. Paris burst into bloom. The streets, more radiant with excitement than usual. The Place de la Concorde, a splendor of French and American flags.

It was there, on that day, that the youngest-ever United States President and his glamorous wife of French extraction would charm and be charmed by the city of Napoleon and Renoir and Claude Debussy . . . and Dietz Edzard. A million Parisians would cheer as Presidents Kennedy and De Gaulle embraced. Not since

Lafayette visited America was there such festivity between the two peoples.

Paris burst into bloom. And that's the way another visitor saw it . . . an art-gallery director from the United States . . . as he stood in the Place de la Concorde. The more he saw the more inspired he became. If only Edzard were here to paint it, he thought. To commemorate this spectacular occasion. But the artist was nearly seventy now. Perhaps battling the crowd would be too great an inconvenience for him.

The gallery director learned differently a few days later, during a meeting with the painter himself. In Edzard's Paris studio they were chatting about art and changing times when the director noticed the painting he had wished for. It was all there . . . the Place de la Concorde, the French and American flags, the excitement of the crowd . . . and something else he had not counted on. Standing to the right, so prominent in the painting that it was almost a portrait of her, was a beautiful dark-haired girl in her mid-twenties. Her eyebrows were arched in an expression too knowing for one so young and her eyes too innocent for one so old. Her complexion was softly blushed cream, and her lips were pink and full. There was a ribbon in her hair and one around her neck, and her dress was the most delicate blue. Gathered in her arms, so lovely yet so diminished by her loveliness, an array of fragile flowers. And the ethereal scent they gave took the gallery director's breath away.

"Who is she?" he asked.

Edzard followed his visitor's gaze to the painting in the corner. "Oh, yes. Of course. I think, of all of them, my favorite model." Then the artist's eyes twinkled like the impressionist stars in the flower girl's dress. "My wife."

The director raised a knowing eyebrow himself. Such a young girl! he thought. And Edzard had married her.

Would his guest like to meet the girl in the painting? It was no sooner said than she entered the studio from the next room, smiled, and kissed her husband.

It might have taken a moment for the artist's visitor to recover from his surprise. Maybe he hasn't yet. But if the portrait of Edzard's wife is enchanted, then is the love they shared also.

The flower girl and the painter's bride were the same. So lovely was she that her presence eclipsed the beauty of the Place de la Concorde and the grandeur of national affairs.

Her beauty, if gone from the eyes of men, was safe in the heart of Dietz Edzard.

For he painted her as he saw her, a girl with the complexion of softly blushed cream, when they'd met . . . in 1927.

37. WAGNER'S COLLABORATOR

Among the most renowned and successful opera composers of all time was Richard Wagner.

His first thirty years marked by failure, historians and musicologists generally concede there was a turn-around time in his career, a point at which Wagner became officially recognized and accepted.

Considering a sudden spark of genius at the age of thirty to have been unlikely, biographers went back to the year 1843 . . . and guess what they found!

In 1843 . . . the year Wagner began writing *Tannhäuser* . . . the theretofore hapless composer took on a collaborator, a trusted critic who aided Wagner in his work.

Why the name of this unsung co-composer does not appear on Wagner's manuscript is THE REST OF THE STORY.

As composers go, Richard Wagner had a late start.

He was already well into his teens before writing music had interested him, and then he began on his own.

He took out a library book on compositional technique, studied the scores of other composers, began lessons on conventional harmony with a neighborhood instructor.

In four years, young Richard began writing an opera called *The Wedding*. The music was so bad he couldn't bear to finish it.

A year later, he began another opera: *The Fairies*. He finished that one, but no one wanted to produce it.

Two more years went by. This time it was an opera called *The Ban on Love*, based on Shakespeare's *Measure for Measure*. The subject matter was racy but not sufficiently intriguing, despite Wagner's music.

It opened and closed the same night.

During these years of musical ill fortune, the composer's financial situation began to deteriorate. He owed money all over Europe, was forever sneaking across borders and sailing away in the dark of night to avoid debtors' prison. He once was even forced to take in lodgers and shine their boots, while he himself stayed home because *his* shoes had no soles.

Still, he continued to write. An opera, *Rienzi*, met with moderate success. Another, *The Flying Dutchman*, didn't quite make it. So Richard Wagner, aged twenty-nine, in debt and disheartened, left town again, and this time moved to Dresden.

And it was in Dresden . . . in 1843 . . . that Wagner's luck changed.

By 1844, *Tannhäuser* had been written. On October 19 of the following year, it was given its premier performance. And Richard Wagner . . . the composer voted least likely to succeed . . . succeeded.

Tannhäuser was a genuine masterpiece . . . and no one knew that its composer had help in writing it!

That's right. When Wagner moved to Dresden . . . when he began writing *Tannhäuser* . . . he was joined by a collaborator . . . an uncelebrated but talented critic.

Now, I should point out that this music critic had no formal training in the art of composition . . . but Wagner so trusted his judgment that the composer dared not enter a single line of music into *Tannhäuser* without first seeking his collaborator's approval.

So it was that composer Wagner enjoyed a certain immortality in his lifetime though his collaborator settled for anonymity. There is no mention of *his* name in Wagner's manuscript . . . perhaps because it might have sounded incredible.

It was incredible that a starving and penniless composer . . . in a last-ditch effort to succeed . . . struck musical gold . . . discarding every melody not approved by his collaborator's *bark!*

I mean, this collaborator would sit behind Wagner's piano bench . . . and when the composer had found the magic combination, the right tune, the collaborator would bark his approval.

One page saved, two pages in the wastebasket . . . and after more than a year, the incomparable *Tannhäuser* was born.

The collaborator?

Peps, Wagner's dog!

38. POLICEWOMAN

An oily midnight mist had settled on the city streets . . . asphalt mirrors from a ten-o'clock rain now past . . . a sleazy street-corner reflection of smog-smudged neon . . . the corner of Sheridan and, incongruously, Sunnyside . . . Chicago.

A lone lady lingers at the curb . . . but no bus will come.

She is Cindy Kane, twenty-eight. Twenty-eight hard years old. Her iridescent dress clings to her slender body. Her face is buried under a technicolor avalanche of makeup.

She is Cindy Kane.

And she has a date.

With someone she has never met . . . and may never meet again.

Minutes have turned to timelessness . . . and a green Chevy four-door pulls slowly around the corner.

The driver's window rolls down. A voice comes from the shadow. . . .

"Are you working?"

Cindy nods . . . regards him with vacant eyes.

He beckons.

She approaches the passenger side. Gets in. And the whole forlorn, unromantic ritual begins all over again. With another stranger.

In the car, Cindy suggests a particular motel.

The driver agrees.

Once in the motel room, Cindy braces herself backward against the dresser.

The stranger speaks. . . .

"Twenty dollars?"

Cindy squints in the bright incandescent light, cocks her head to one side. . . . "I'm sorry, I didn't hear you. What did you say?"

"I said, 'twenty dollars' . . . is twenty dollars all right?" He extends a folded twenty-dollar bill to Cindy.

She takes the bill . . . and the reality behind the rendezvous is abruptly revealed.

A closet door slams open.

Two police officers emerge from their hiding place.

The mirror on the door . . . is a two-way mirror.

Cindy draws a compact semiautomatic from her purse.

"You're under arrest," says Cindy Kane calmly. And rights are recited.

For you see, sleazy Cindy Kane . . . is a policewoman.

No one ever expected Cindy Kane to become a policewoman.

As a teen-ager, she was a quiet girl. Later she became a part-time social worker at a Chicago youth shelter. Troubled youngsters. Their families.

But it was at the shelter, that Cindy Kane became unsheltered. One of the youngsters in Cindy's care had come from Iowa to visit her aunt in the big city. At the Greyhound station she was met by a pimp who got her away . . . got her on drugs . . . got her "in the business."

Missing for two and a half months, the girl showed up at the shelter . . . beaten black and blue . . . and then Cindy knew . . . there was something more she could do.

So Cindy Kane . . . became a policewoman.

She subjected herself to life's seamy side for the sake of the countless, nameless victims . . . like the little girl from Iowa.

Cindy is a streetwalker decoy . . . a mock high-class call girl to bust rings run by low-life businessmen . . . a pretend prostitute-housewife . . . a bait to drag drug dealers from their lairs.

She's been threatened, beaten bloody, and come back for more, because Cindy Kane is not just a policewoman . . . she's a *good* policewoman.

At one time, she was even more than that.

For if the incongruity strikes you that a sweet young thing with a kind heart should purposely, professionally place herself among scum . . . then hear the whole truth about Cindy Kane.

Just six years ago, at the age of twenty-two, Cindy Kane was not Cindy Kane at all.

Cindy was Sister Mary Anthony . . . at Our Lady of the Good Shepherd Convent . . . a Roman Catholic nun.

And now you know THE REST OF THE STORY.

Of all the artists and musicians with proud and exotic names, perhaps none was so proud . . . so apparently exotic . . . as pianist Olga Samaroff.

She confounded audiences on two continents with legendary performances of the Tchaikovsky First Piano Concerto, with dazzling recitals of piano music that spanned the centuries. In fact she, Olga Samaroff, is considered by a majority of critics to have had the most brilliant career . . . and the longest . . . of all her contemporaries.

She was herself for two years a music critic on the New York *Evening Post*. And her impact offstage was felt elsewhere. She taught at the Juilliard Graduate School and at the Philadelphia Conservatory. Among her best-known pupils were William Kapell and Rosalyn Tureck.

But it is for her charismatic, enigmatic life on the concert stage that Olga Samaroff is best remembered. She performed at a time when Russian musicians were enormously popular, but Olga Samaroff by any other name would have been a great pianist.

The first woman from her native country to be admitted to the Paris Conservatoire, she studied there before returning to America in 1900.

And American audiences must have been intrigued indeed by

her authority, by her bearing . . . and by that almost magical name, Olga Samaroff.

Wherever she went in the world, Olga Samaroff created a sensation. She was a formidable woman . . . a fiery and temperamental pianist . . . and perhaps to some she was even cloaked in mystery.

During an age when Russian artists were particularly in demand, Olga Samaroff was particularly in demand . . . but she was not Russian.

If the pseudonym Samaroff was enough to intrigue her audiences, it was also enough to intrigue the man whom she would one day marry: Maestro Leopold Stokowski. Whether she told him THE REST OF THE STORY when they first met, only they would know.

For Olga Samaroff was born in San Antonio.

Her name, before it was Mme. Leopold Stokowski . . . before it was Olga Samaroff . . . was Lucy Hickenlooper.

40. PELORUS JACK

The story books are filled with retired sailors . . . with old salts whose ships have come to port while their mistress is forever the sea. So they sink their savings into a secondhand tug, and escort the big ships, and reminisce, till their days are done.

One such story, a strange and tender one, comes from New Zealand. And the story is true.

Cook Straight separates the North and South islands of New Zealand. Halfway through, there is an inlet, a treacherously narrow passageway called Pelorus Sound.

For ships attempting to navigate Pelorus Sound, there was always the danger of the rocks . . . until the old sailor came. He had left the life of the open sea behind, to live out his days guiding other sailors through hazardous Pelorus Sound.

His name was Jack.

Picture old Jack out there waiting by the dock for the next big ship to leave. He never asked for pay. He never petitioned the shipyards to put him on the payroll. Jack just figured he'd had his day at sea, and no one knew the rocks and bars of Pelorus Sound better than he. It was his labor of love. Guiding the giant vessels out to the safety of Cook Straight was his way of saying to the younger, less experienced sailors, "Learn from me!"

From the decks of the big ships, the crewmen would call out, "Hey, Jack! Fair weather today?"

But old Jack never said much. Perhaps there would be a friendly wave, and that recognition was quite enough.

There would never be an old sailors' home for Pelorus Jack, the pilot of the sound. The other old sea dogs could give up if they wanted to. But Jack would stay at work. All day. Every day. And sometimes late into the night.

When he rested, it was close enough to hear the gentle surging of the surf. When he ate, he fished his breakfast from the deep waters of Cook Straight. Of all New Zealand sailors, none more than he was at one with the sea.

Then, one December morning, the mistress claimed her lover. And Pelorus Jack sank beneath the whitecaps of Cook Straight, gone forever, home at last.

When news got out that Jack was missing at sea, there was a season of mourning on the sound. But the younger, the less experienced, were older, wiser now. From Pelorus Jack they'd learned the water and the rocks, and they remembered.

And a few remembered an ancient legend from the cliffs of the South Island. New Zealand draws its wealth of folklore from the Maori culture. The story has it that two young Maori tribesmen once sought the hand of the same maiden. When the maiden at last chose one, the rejected suitor broke into a rage. After his wrath had been vented, the bodies of the maiden and her intended lay lifeless on the beach of Pelorus Sound. But the murderer would not go unpunished. For the tribal curse he received would condemn him to a reincarnation . . . as the pilot of Pelorus Sound . . . as the mariner who was forever after to guide others through the treacherous water.

Whether Pelorus Jack, the real-life mariner who for a quarter of a century lived out that legend—whether he ever heard the Maori tale is anyone's guess.

Most would guess not. For Pelorus Jack had spent his life at sea, far away from land lovers' stories. When he retired to the sound, it was only to help. Or was he merely the last link in a watery chain, the pawn of an ancient Maori incantation?

No one really knew where Jack came from or, for that matter, where he went when he disappeared.

Although Jack really lived, if the legend is true he settled an old score . . . took the rap for a murder committed a thousand years before.

There was a postscript to that ancient curse, and that also was true. For Pelorus Jack . . . the real-life pilot of the sound . . . the perhaps unwitting party to a long-past incantation . . . was a dolphin.

41. MR. "NICE GUY"

This story is rated "R." Due to mature subject matter, the true story you're about to hear may not be suitable for, well . . . for just anyone.

We're going to talk about a fellow named Bram Stoker. He was a prominent theater manager during the Victorian era. And we're going to talk about his wife. Then we're going to talk about the one un-special, predictably Victorian difficulty between them.

Bram Stoker was a genuinely gentle man.

He was general manager of the celebrated Lyceum Theatre Company, and those in his employ described him as "one of the most kind and tenderhearted men, filling a difficult position with great tact."

Everywhere he went, Bram Stoker drew that sort of reaction. He was a sweet guy, they say, an easy goer and a getter along.

As is often the case with nice fellows, he had a problem he never talked about . . . a family problem, one of those touchy things.

Bram had married a woman named Florence Balcombe, one of the great beauties of her time. A photograph or two survive her, so we know her attractiveness was not a myth. At any rate, she was courted by everyone who was anyone . . . even Oscar Wilde, another Victorian luminary. But in the end Florence wound up with Bram Stoker. Good old, easygoing Bram.

This marriage of theirs couldn't have looked better. The handsome young theater manager and his beautiful young wife were adored as the darling couple of society. Then came the birth of their only child, Noel, and the fairy-tale quality of their romance seemed consummate.

We're not going to judge Florence too harshly here. After all, we really don't know her that well. For the time being, we'll suppose that childbirth was difficult for her, so difficult, perhaps, that the thought of bearing future children was unbearable. Anyway, for whatever reason, the biographers tell us Florence lost her love for Bram and, because of her indifference, affection ceased between them.

Now, remember, this is good old, undemanding, easygoing Bram. This is the Bram Stoker who was known for his honesty, the Bram Stoker who gave to his friends without asking in return. So you know why he would never demand affection from his wife . . . why he would not complain to her . . . or to anyone, for that matter. And that's why, from all outward appearances, Bram's marriage remained intact.

But it was not intact. The truth would come out, one day, in a very sad way. And the latent hostility of a nice guy who felt himself finishing last . . . his submerged feelings . . . would surface, too.

Bram Stoker and his wife would continue to live their celebrated life. With friends like Walt Whitman and Mark Twain and Teddy Roosevelt, they could expect the heat of the limelight.

But at night . . .

At night Bram Stoker became . . . someone else. For the problems he could or would not work out at home, he sought to solve otherwise.

Bram died, in his sixties, of syphilis. He left the world the shattered illusion of a one-time fairy-tale romance . . . and he also left a book.

For Bram Stoker was an author, too. Although we've forgotten about him as such, no one will ever forget the monster that grew out of his ill-fated marriage.

He is with us still as the character women dared not, could not resist.

For tenderhearted, undemanding Bram Stoker exhumed that buried resentment toward his wife in his private life . . . in a book about it.

The book you never knew till now was an allegorical autobiography. For in his fantasy Bram extended the dimensions of his philandering in the character of aggressive, demanding *Dracula*.

42. NAPOLEON OF THE WEST

Of all the men Texas admires most . . . of all the state forefathers whose memories are cherished . . . none rides taller in the saddle than Sam Houston.

He was an Easterner, in fact, born in Virginia. And he was not a consistent hero. Before his life was through, he'd had many ups and downs. But few whom Texas has claimed for its own, measure up to the legend of Sam Houston. Because the legend is true. Because if it were not for Sam, Texas would be Mexican.

There was another living legend in early Texas history . . . a self-styled "Napoleon of the West": General Santa Anna. With victories at Goliad and the Alamo under his *bandolera*, Santa Anna's claim on the territory that is now Texas seemed assured.

As commander in chief of the Texan army, Sam Houston was called to do battle with Santa Anna . . . to win the Texas territory. The Texan and the Mexican armies would meet at San Jacinto.

For the only time in his entire military career, General Sam Houston called a council of war. Should they attack or wait to be attacked? That was the question. Sam listened as his advisers discussed and debated and theorized, getting noplace. When the others had had their say, General Sam looked at his watch. It was 3:30 P.M. He dismissed the council, he issued the order: attack!

The battle of San Jacinto began at four o'clock. You'll want to make note of that. The Texan commander raised his sword . . . the fife and drum played "Come to the Bower" . . . and the last army of the Texas Republic moved up from the woods and across the sloping plain.

It was a swashbuckling spectacle that torrid Texas afternoon . . . the silken flag of liberty flying in the wind, the glove of some first lieutenant's sweetheart bobbing from its staff.

There was no opposition at first. None.

There was Sam . . . charging down the center on his splendid white stallion, waving his troops toward the enemy encampment.

Then the first enemy volley thundered. Sam's white stallion went down. But General Sam, blood filling his boot, threw himself onto a cavalryman's pony and resumed his patrol of the line.

"Remember the Alamo!"

His battle cry ripped the sky. Then a shout from somewhere in the rear. . . .

"Fight for your lives! The bridge has been cut!"

The bridge. Their only avenue of retreat. For the Texans, it was now a fight to the death. Knives drawn, the infantry slashed ahead . . . into and over torn barricades.

Seven hundred and forty-three Texans. Sixteen hundred Mexicans. But the Mexican force was in such disarray, so unready, I guess you could say, that General Sam, keeping them off balance, waded into them. He drove them into the marsh . . . and in minutes the battle was over. Santa Anna was defeated. Texas . . . was Texas.

Today, nearly a century and a half later, that marsh has become a lake. The San Jacinto battleground is sinking, they say, and the surrounding bay may someday swallow it whole. But if those defeated Mexicans who were shoved into the swamp could come up for air just one more time, they might tell you what really happened that April day at San Jacinto.

The "Napoleon of the West" was crushed in a battle that lasted less than twenty minutes. For Sam's decision to attack was strategy timed to the clock. Though his troops were outnumbered by more than two to one, the decisive factor was in his favor.

For Sam Houston knew what Santa Anna did . . . at 4 P.M. And he caught Santa Anna, literally, sleeping.

Queen Victoria was among the most popular rulers in British history.

The Victorian era was named for her.

She called many mansions home.

Kensington, where she was born.

Buckingham, where she ruled.

But of all the Queen's mansions, one was by far the most curious and chilling.

That was the place where she died. That was Osborne House. Osborne House, the Queen's winter home on the Isle of Wight.

Only Queen Victoria visited the darkened rooms upstairs, only she knew what besides empty silence was there.

And then she died.

And then, the few who discovered her secret, aghast, were hesitant to say what they had found.

For they had learned what you are about to learn: THE REST OF THE STORY.

Victoria, Queen of Great Britain, Queen of Ireland, Empress of India. The Victorian age, which included the greater part of the 1800s, was hers. It was a time of industrial expansion for England, and imperial expansion for her territories. A period of sentiment and self-indulgence was over. The English people became high-minded, modest, self-righteous, enterprising. Behind it all was Victoria, their Queen.

She ruled for sixty-three years, longer than any other British monarch. She took the throne at a time when the throne itself was neither loved nor respected. But Victoria, *by being herself above reproach*, elevated that royal position to unprecedented heights. Perhaps the throne is there today because of her.

During that eventful reign, Britain fought the Opium War in China, the Crimean War, the Boer War. There were numerous small rebellions in Canada, assorted skirmishes with the Chinese, the Abyssinians, the Afghans, the Zulus. Through it all, Victoria held her empire, and her people, together.

During the Victorian era, the colonies in British North America and Australia were federated and became self-governing. Britain herself became a free-trade country. In Ireland, the Anglican Church was disestablished and the land system was reformed. At home Parliament passed acts improving labor conditions, making education compulsory, reforming the civil service. Above and behind and within it all, was Queen Victoria.

Her marriage to Prince Albert was among history's happiest marriages. Out of it grew nine children—four sons and five daughters.

The Prince Consort was a student, a philanthropist, a businessman. He, too, was well loved. Especially by his Queen.

In 1861, Prince Albert died.

Victoria never recovered from her grief. For many years she dressed in mourning, became affectionately known as "The Widow of Windsor." She never slept in a bed that did not have his picture by its side. Till the day she died. In the winter of 1901. At Osborne House.

The Victorian era had passed away into night. What at last came out into the light . . . was the secret of those darkened upstairs rooms . . . the rooms that only she visited.

But now Edward was King, Victoria's son. He ascended the stairs of that sprawling estate . . . and threw open the doors.

What he saw made him weak . . . turned him pale . . . turned him away.

For what Edward the King had discovered represented a lifetime of self-torment . . . his mother's private collection . . . of photographs.

Hundreds of photographs . . . of four generations . . . of friends and relatives.

And each of these photos had a startling similarity.

For all of the hundreds of faces in the gruesome gallery of Queen Victoria . . . were corpses . . . photographed at their own funerals.

It was a party for teen-agers, and Addie felt out of place. Even in his own home.

Addie was only twelve, but his older sister asked him to "stick around."

So he stuck around.

It was a snowy December evening outside, and Addie longed to go "coasting," as he called it. But the other party attendants were much too preoccupied with their own games and their own conversations. He would have to wait for another time.

Then one of the older boys, who'd been away at school, noticed Addie, alone, staring gloomily out the window.

"Say, Addie!" he said. "I learned the manual of arms last semester!"

Addie's ears perked up. The manual of arms! That was what they did in the army drill, wasn't it?

Would Addie like to see how it went? The older boy wanted to know. All they needed was a rifle.

Well, Addie's folks had a .22 rifle in the hall closet. That would do!

So Addie brought him the gun, and the boy gave a quick demonstration.

Accounts of what happened next vary. After the older boy

showed Addie the manual of arms, some say Addie was trying to imitate it. Others say he was about to put the rifle away. But one eyewitness swears that Addie took the gun from the older boy . . . pointed it at one of the girls . . . and pulled the trigger.

The gun was loaded. And a young girl . . . Ruth Merwin . . . fell to the library floor . . . dead.

Addie dropped the rifle, and his eyes widened to see blood pouring from Ruth's forehead. He turned on his heel and ran upstairs to his room, alone.

The snow was still falling outside, more heavily now. One of the youngsters left to fetch Ruth Merwin's parents. The party was over.

The aftermath was as curious as the incident was tragic. No one in Addie's family, so far as we know, ever mentioned Ruth Merwin's death. Addie himself would not speak of it until many years had passed. In fact, three weeks after the accident, Addie wrote his father a letter in which he mentions the Merwin family . . . but nowhere in that letter is there a trace of remorse . . . or even the slightest indication that anything had happened.

Armchair psychologists like to theorize that Addie's later devotion to "causes" is traced back to guilt associated with the shattering occurrence in his childhood. But this is probably a shallow interpretation of a complex personality.

Still, Addie was haunted for the rest of his life by self-doubt and feelings of unworthiness.

As a man, when honors were bestowed upon him by his peers, Addie would accept reluctantly, saying, "I should have preferred to hear those words uttered for a stronger, a wiser, a better man than myself."

But honors would continue to be bestowed upon him.

And Addie would continue to be plagued by vague melancholy feelings. It was not unusual for him to begin a letter to a friend with such a phrase as "It is very late and I am propped up in bed, desolate, weary, harassed and sad."

So one gunshot on a long-past, snowy December evening echoed throughout Addie's life, though his own wife would have to learn from a friend of this incident in her husband's childhood.

Addie was always known as a gentle man, quiet and mild-mannered. Those who had not learned of that cryptic chapter in his life would never have associated Addie with violence of any kind.

On the wings of a peaceful image, he rose to a revered position, came to be respected and admired . . . all the while turning a guilt-deafened ear to adulation.

For the honor he would have preferred to see a better man receive . . . was the Democratic presidential nomination of 1952.

The man who lived his life for others . . . Addie . . . was Adlai Stevenson. And now you know his REST OF THE STORY.

45. DRAG-STRIP SIMPSON

Drag-Strip Simpson once said that he never wanted to get out of anything as much as he wanted to get out of his job.

Now, if Simpson's profession had been drag racing, he wouldn't have said that.

He enjoyed nothing better than to take his wheels out on the open road . . . or for that matter, on a city street . . . and peel away as if there were no tomorrow!

But he hated his job.

Oh, yes . . . he hated something else too . . . his real first name . . . Hiram.

He intentionally dropped the name Hiram when he started school. Coincidentally, it was around that time Simpson developed his lust for speed.

But now he was a grown man. And he still couldn't resist a drag race.

Hiram Simpson had quite a reputation with the police.

It was nothing to discover him, on a given day, challenging to a drag race some unsuspecting soul stopped at an urban intersection.

Simpson's record included: April 11, '66, arrested for speeding. Fine paid at precinct court.

July 1, same year, arrested for speeding. Fine paid at precinct court. He promised it would not happen again.

It happened again.

As a matter of fact, it happened again right after Hiram took the new job I was telling you about . . . the one he hated.

Simpson was racing west, on a major thoroughfare between Eleventh and Twelfth, when he was spotted by a pedestrian, Bill West. This in itself wouldn't have been so unfortunate for Simpson, had it not been for one thing: Bill West was a police officer walking his beat!

Now, the officer had no walkie-talkie . . . he couldn't contact a traffic patrolman . . . but when he saw Simpson flashing down the street like a bolt of lightning on wheels, he knew he had to do something.

So Officer West, in a moment of reckless daring, lunged for the speeding vehicle . . . and hung on!

At once, Drag-Strip Simpson heard the frantic cries of the policeman: "Stop! Stop!"

Simpson stopped.

Officer West, who had been dragged for about fifty feet, picked himself up, regained his composure.

Hiram began to apologize. Then he requested that the officer do his duty.

The officer did his duty.

Simpson was arrested. His hot-rod was impounded. He posted a bond, which he later forfeited because he didn't show up for the trial.

Oh, but he *did* write a nice letter to the police commissioner . . . commending Officer Bill West's bravery in the line of duty.

If you consider any of these events to be most remarkable, you must also consider that we're talking about a most remarkable man.

Hiram "Drag-Strip" Simpson.

He once said that he never wanted to get out of anything as much as he wanted to get out of his job.

Maybe he was trying to get fired. Who knows?

But one thing's certain. Eventually he settled into that job, made his mark . . . and perhaps only occasionally missed the adventure of his first profession, army general.

Some overlook his traffic record. They say he was just getting used to being . . . the President of the United States . . . Hiram Ulysses Simpson Grant.

And now you know THE REST OF THE STORY.

46. THE GOATHERD WHO MADE IT TO THE DICTIONARY

César's mother adored her son's hands. How beautifully made they were! she'd always say. Surely young César would someday become an artist.

After all, there'd been a painter in the family, generations before. And an altar carver.

But alas, most of César's ancestors were goatherds, and his father was a goatherd.

So the boy with the hands of an artist became instead a herder of goats.

César lived in a tiny Swiss village of fewer than two hundred people, the thirteenth child of a peasant couple. His father, Anton, owned a few cows and goats, and in the summer, when school was out, César helped Papa herd them.

Mama and Papa disagreed over furthering César's education. Papa said it would be a waste of time. Mama was ambitious for her children. César himself did not know what he wanted to do.

"Would you not like to be an artist? Or an engineer?" she asked him.

César said he preferred herding the goats.

That was two to one against Mama.

But Mama won.

When he was twelve, César was sent to Sion. There he would

learn French and mathematics. At the end of three years he had not learned French or mathematics. And he still preferred herding the goats.

Now Papa Anton was upset. Perhaps César *should* have a chance at life beyond their little home cradled up against the mountains. So Papa wrote to a friend who owned a hotel in a nearby town. He sent along three hundred francs and a plea to give his young son a job.

The friend wrote back and the deal was settled. César became an apprentice wine waiter at the hotel.

At first the boy was eager to learn. He tried his very best. But somehow he just couldn't get the hang of it.

And it frustrated him.

It frustrated him so much that he began dropping wine corks in the clients' soup, bumping into and knocking over whole trays of *crudités*, the raw vegetables he served as appetizers.

The hotel manager became frustrated. Then he became angry. Then he gave up. At last he called young César into his office and gave him the facts straight out:

"Boy," he said, "I'm quite fond of your father, but there is a point at which friendship ceases. I told him I'd give you a try, and I gave you a try, but now I must give you a piece of advice and I hope you will listen. Go back to your Papa. Go back to your goat herds and be happy in the life you were meant to lead. You will never make anything of yourself in the hotel business. It requires a special flair, and I must tell you the truth . . . you do not have it."

César managed to stifle the tears until after he left the manager's office. For the first time in his young life, he'd failed at something he really wanted to do. And now he was faced with the prospect of returning home and disappointing his hopeful parents.

César did not return home, so there is THE REST OF THE STORY.

He'd been dismissed from his job as a hotel waiter, but he was too proud to admit defeat.

Instead he went to Paris . . . and from there went on—and on —one day to see his name in the dictionary!

Yes, César had been told most emphatically that he would never make anything of himself in the hotel business. But for almost a hundred years the hotel business has been trying to live up to him.

He began as a herder of goats—nothing more—yet lived to see the world's most elegant hotels wear his simple peasant name.

That name is engraved in gold and enshrined in the dictionary as a four-letter synonym for elegance.

Anything so labeled is the ultimate in refined opulence.

To this day the world tips its hat at the very mention of the family name of César—RITZ.

47. ESCAPE!

Of all the positions in the field of journalism, that of war correspondent is perhaps most dangerous. Some are captured, some escape. Some die.

Twenty-five-year-old Leonard Spencer was the London *Morning Post's* newest correspondent. His assignment was the Boer War, in South Africa.

Had young Leonard foreseen the peril awaiting him, he would probably have taken the assignment anyway. That's how Leonard was.

About twenty miles from Ladysmith, Leonard could hear the booming guns. He was aboard a British armored train that would take him as close to the front as he could get.

The train got too close. There was a sudden crash. The train had struck a boulder on the tracks . . . a Boer booby trap. It was an ambush!

Immediately, a fusillade of rifle fire followed. Surprised, British troops on the train fired back.

And Leonard? Leonard ignored the gunshots and exploding shells. He jumped off the train, directed the British defense, helped to clear the wreckage.

In fact, without the aid of this youthful correspondent from the

Morning Post, the train might well have been lost and the British troops massacred.

Instead, the wreckage was cleared, the train *did* pull out of the trap and carried a good many British soldiers with it.

The one left behind to face the enemy . . . was Leonard! No, the story does not end sadly there.

Leonard was captured, unharmed. Even though Leonard was technically a war correspondent, the Boer commander was sufficiently impressed with his bravery . . . to have Leonard thrown into prison at Pretoria.

The Pretoria prison was among the world's most carefully guarded strongholds. Still, that did not stop Leonard from plotting an escape with two other British captives.

As darkness fell, the trio waited for their opportunity. It was now pitch black. The sentries exchanged their posts. Leonard sprang across an open area, hurdled a fence of barbed-wire mesh. When he looked back, there was no one. His comrades had missed their chance!

Three hundred miles of hostile territory lay between Leonard and his freedom. For a while, he followed the railroad tracks to the east, stumbling alone, through the dark, dodging enemy patrols. Tired, hungry, thirsty . . . Leonard plodded long into the night, knowing that, each painful foot of the way, one false step could be his last.

The night turned to day and back to night again, until the days and nights blurred.

Finally Leonard reached a mining town. His luck wearing thin but holding, he knocked on the door of the only Britisher in the territory and was smuggled onto a train loaded with bales of wool.

The train would carry him to the British consul. To safety.

And that's how Leonard Spencer, the London *Morning Post's* fledgling correspondent, got his story . . . and his reputation for daring.

History has all but forgotten this incident in his life in order to make room for later glory.

The fortune that once seemed to be wearing thin had only begun . . . and one day rubbed off on all of England.

For the young correspondent who once upon a time saved a British armored train and escaped the enemy under impossible circumstances . . . continued to do the impossible for the rest of his life.

We knew him as *Sir* Winston Leonard Spencer Churchill!

And now you know THE REST OF THE STORY.

Henri Latour was to France what Sherlock Holmes had been to England. Only, Henri Latour was real . . . a real-life detective who seemed always to get his man. So hailed was he, in this respect, that Latour even while he lived was a legend.

If the legend has been enhanced, embellished in the years since his death . . . no amount of truth-stretching could be more remarkable than the hard, cold facts surrounding his last case.

Master sleuth Henri Latour was called to the scene of the crime.

A suspect had already been taken into custody. Instinctively, supersleuth Latour said, no . . . the authorities had arrested the wrong man.

How could Latour be so certain? police wanted to know.

It was a matter of simple deduction, the detective assured them. Pieces were missing from the puzzle. He, Latour, would find the pieces . . . would unravel the tangled clues. He, Latour, would lead them to the true criminal.

So began what some described as the most brilliant track-down in the history of France. Carefully, Latour assembled the fragmented evidence, one piece, one step, at a time.

It was a heinous crime which Latour was investigating, and

somewhere in the darkened pathways of a complex maze a particularly heinous criminal waited.

An elderly couple had been robbed, brutally murdered. Citizens, from behind their locked doors, were comforted to hear that Latour was on the case . . . that Latour was closing in.

And Latour was closing in.

Perhaps, one day, it would be the trace of blood on a scarf . . . and the next, a chip of knife steel extracted from human bone.

The days became weeks . . . until enough evidence was accumulated to clear the suspect who was in custody. The proof was positive, declared detective Latour. The man police had apprehended . . . must now be set free.

Shouldn't he be held a while longer, authorities asked, just in case? Just in case the master sleuth, if for the first time, this time was wrong?

But Latour was not wrong, he assured them again. An innocent man had been charged, and no innocent man should be forced to pay for the crimes of the guilty.

The search continued.

More evidence was gathered . . . one piece . . . one painfully slow step at a time.

Perhaps now it was a torn patch of tweed . . . or a smudge on a railing . . . but Latour was closing in.

One day, the search ended. The puzzle pieces had fallen into place. At the end of a long road . . . a long and arduous journey . . . Latour found his man.

The trial was not a lengthy one, for the case was ironclad. Latour was on hand personally to reweave an amazing web for the jury . . . and the verdict was "guilty."

The judge commended Latour for his tireless effort . . . for his brilliant detective work. The newspapers applauded.

But with that verdict—abruptly—without explanation—Latour retired, went into seclusion.

Everyone agreed that last track-down had been his greatest triumph.

Yet the Sherlock Holmes of Paris would live the final twenty-five years of his life . . . as a hermit . . . as a recluse in a lonely little cottage in a remote French village.

Only after his death would the carefully guarded secret come to light—and an admiring nation learn the whole truth about Latour's last case.

For the innocent stranger whom Latour had set free was—alas—but an innocent stranger.

When the last piece of the puzzle was in place, the dedicated detective was himself trapped by his own uncompromising sense of justice.

For he had by then been led, by the evidence he had so arduously collected, to the arrest and conviction of his own son.

What you're about to hear is going to sound a lot like a Horatio Alger story. In fact, this *is* the Horatio Alger story.

Horatio Alger, you remember, was the author who wrote all those success stories about fictional characters like Ragged Dick. The whole rags-to-riches idea is almost synonymous with Alger.

You can imagine that this immensely successful author mirrored the success of his book characters in his own life. And because of Horatio Alger's twofold success . . . fiction and fact . . . generations of youth have been inspired by the notion that a poor boy with perseverance can become a millionaire.

In many ways Horatio Alger *is* the American dream, so much so that he's been credited by some as singlehandedly spurring the Industrial Revolution in the United States.

So here's the story of a poor boy . . . born into an unhealthy, unhappy childhood on a Friday the thirteenth . . . who rose to become one of the most entirely successful and highly paid authors of all time.

This is the Horatio Alger story. From birth he was undersize, underweight, susceptible to every imaginable childhood disease. In an age of comparatively primitive medicines and remedies, it's a miracle that he survived infancy.

At two, Horatio developed a severe asthmatic condition. He

was kept apart from other children through most of his youth. Overawed and perhaps intimidated by his father, a stern New England preacher, he was slow to talk, and when he talked, he stuttered.

As a young boy, Horatio's only friends were books. He seemed to develop his mind to compensate for a frail and undependable body.

At sixteen he passed the entrance exams at Harvard. But his family was unable to foot the bill, so Horatio had to work his way through school.

He became errand boy for the university president. That entitled him to a free room and a dollar a week. It wasn't enough. Horatio entered an essay contest . . . and won . . . and the prize money kept him going for a while.

During vacation he earned money by teaching in country schools. Confidence crept into his life at last. He became able to support himself. His Harvard peers applauded his scholastic achievements. His writing improved. And by graduation, every trace of a once bewildered and sickly boy had disappeared. He overcame his awkward, tongue-tied past and delivered his commencement oration without a stutter.

When it came to his profession as writer, Horatio still had a difficult climb ahead of him. He wrote dozens of articles and received dozens of rejections. When at last publishers accepted a piece or two, there was no pay.

Finally, professional recognition. Two dollars . . . for three poems. Hardly a living.

It would take years of determination for Horatio Alger's storybook success. Four years till his first collection of short stories was published . . . twelve years for his first novel. But once he got his foot in the door, the perseverance paid off.

In a short while, his yearly earnings would be comparable to a quarter of a million dollars today. Writing up to seven books a year, he soon became the most popular of popular authors. Some say the best-selling American author of all time.

And each of those inspiring books was a variation on a theme . . . a prototype of his first successful novel, *Ragged Dick.* All of Alger's fictional heroes were much like the original Dick Hunter, a boy bootblack on the streets of New York who rose from rags to riches on the wings of honesty, hard work, and a little bit of luck.

Perhaps Horatio Alger believed himself to be Dick Hunter. His success was no less astounding and every bit as earned. So for generations of young Dick Hunters, Horatio Alger became the beloved embodiment of the American dream.

The American dream is still good. Don't let anyone tell you different. But as in any dream, our confidence comes from the confidence of our heroes.

Horatio Alger was our hero. His success spurred us on. He was our mirror, reflecting the positive possibilities in the lives of all of us.

Yet few knew that Horatio Alger . . . the striving young author who climbed to the summit of his profession . . . the man who for a century symbolized success . . . had in real life clawed his way from rags to riches . . . only to return to rags.

You see, Horatio Alger . . . died broke.

50. WILLEM'S PASSION

More than anything, Willem wanted to be an evangelist. He was only twenty-five, a century ago, but already he'd been an art dealer, language teacher, bookseller . . . and unsuccessful in love.

But more than all the paintings and all the words and all the books and all the women, Willem wanted to devote himself to his fellow man, and the Word of God.

It was this passion that brought young Willem, in the spring of 1879, to the coal fields of southern Belgium. It was there, in a little mining town, that Willem outlined THE REST OF THE STORY on the back of a faded envelope.

Perhaps it was the young minister's total selflessness that first captured the respect of the miners in that tiny Borinage community. In a mine disaster, scores of the villagers were injured and no one fought harder to save them than he.

Day and night, Willem nursed the wounded, fed the hungry, clothed the poor. He even scraped the slag heaps to give his people fuel.

After the rubble was cleared and the dead were buried and the sick were made well, the townspeople turned to the Dutchman who had healed their physical hurts . . . and adopted him as their spiritual leader.

Every Sunday they overflowed Willem's services to hear this unassuming man preach the literal Word of God. And then light-ning struck.

A visiting church official discovered Willem living in a simple hut, dressed in an old soldier's coat and trousers made of sacking. When he asked Willem what he had done with his salary, Wil-lem answered simply that he'd given it to the miners.

The church official told Willem that he looked more miserable than the people he taught. Why had he given everything away? Willem asked, wasn't this what Christ had intended for his disci-ples?

"There's such a thing as too literally interpreting the Scrip-tures," the church official argued. He went on to say that the con-ventions Willem had destroyed would take years to rebuild.

Willem was dismissed from the service of the church that day. He was devastated. The career that had meant everything was suddenly nothing. There followed weeks of despair.

Then, one afternoon, Willem noticed an old miner. He was bending beneath the enormous weight of a full sack of coal. In that instant, Willem again felt the desperation of these people . . . and recognized that it would always be his own.

Fumbling through his pockets, the Dutchman pulled out a tat-tered envelope . . . and then a pencil . . . and began to sketch the weary figure that had moved him so. That first drawing was a crude one, but he tried over and over again.

Beginning that day, Willem was to capture for the world the torment, triumph, and dignity of the people he loved.

If Willem had failed as a minister, there was now a new passion . . . a new purpose.

And the people he was not allowed to teach, he was able to reach through art. In the process he immortalized them . . . and they him.

For the end of Willem's career as a clergyman motivated a min-istry more monumental than he had ever dreamed.

Because the preacher who wasn't to be, became the artist the world would know . . . as Vincent Willem van Gogh.

51. LITTLE BOOK LOST

Delicate-featured, mild-mannered author Clarence Shepard was dying at a time that his work was coming alive.

Aged sixty, his career had begun only fifteen years before. And they'd been hard years. One book followed the other with lukewarm success.

At last, Clarence had hit on something. His next book would surely be a best seller . . . and, probably, his last.

That's all I'm going to tell you about him right now. Because the slender volume he submitted from his deathbed carried with it THE REST OF THE STORY.

Clarence's book was lost.

The manuscript had been received by the publisher . . . sent to the printer . . . but when no proofs were returned, the publisher became anxious. One telephone call explained it all.

It seems that the text had arrived at the printer's. But it was so thin . . . inobtrusively wrapped in brown paper. Somehow, someone had mislaid it, discarded it.

And so began a publisher's exhaustive search. If this only copy of the manuscript was gone forever, how could they face the dying author with the news?

Lead number one: Most of the printer's discarded paper was sent to a warehouse in Boston. The searchers sped to the warehouse. Confronted with a mountain of scrap paper, they riffled through it one leaf at a time. The book was not there.

Lead number two: Some of the printer's waste was sent to a mill in Connecticut. Perhaps the little text was in that batch. The searchers arrived at the mill. Three days of scouring proved hopeless. Still no book.

Lead number three: An apprentice back at the print shop remembered that a small bale of scrap was delivered a few days ago to a Massachusetts mill. That had to be it. So the weary manuscript hunters went there, believing their job to be almost finished. It had only started.

The bale had been received . . . thrown in the hopper. The machinery that spewed paper from this huge dumping bin into an acid tank could not be stopped. Certainly not for a few ounces of paper, anyway.

The searchers posted themselves at the mouth of the chute, in shifts, around the clock. Their only hope was to snag Clarence's manuscript as it flew out on its way to oblivion.

No one remembers how long the vigil continued. Certainly the fatigue and growing discouragement of the hunters blurred their sense of time. But it was long enough for them to give in to despair . . . to abandon their mission. It was all over except to tell Clarence.

That's when the last-posted search-party member turned around quickly . . . spied a small brown paper package flying from the chute. Nearly tumbling into the acid tank himself, he lunged for the little parcel . . . and recovered it.

Author Clarence Shepard was dying at a time that his work was coming alive. But he'd never really meant to be a writer. At first it was merely a means of passing a long and difficult confinement to his bed.

Stricken forever with crippling arthritis in his mid-twenties, Clarence would be an invalid for another twenty until his first book was published. Fifteen more years would go by until he was able to paint with words the gentle portrait from his past that pleasantly haunted him.

That's why the little book lost was so precious . . . to an author whose quiet memories eased the bitterness of endless illness . . .

to a world that watched those memories come to life in print and on the stage.

The little book found that made us smile . . . that brightened the long night of Clarence Shepard Day . . . was to run for an unprecedented three thousand performances on Broadway.

Life with Father.

52. WE'RE GOING TO MAKE YOU A STAR

The path from anonymity to stardom is almost always Under Construction. Sometimes it's a dead end. Sometimes it's deceptively paved with fool's gold. Still, if the Yellow Brick Road were a superhighway, there'd be more of us on the screen than in the theater, and that just couldn't be.

The movie business is glutted with ten-year overnight successes . . . actors and actresses who've paid their dues by haunting the casting lines for bit parts in cheap productions while part-timing as store clerks and waitresses. Then a small break. And a larger one. And a larger one until the shock wave hits and the name nobody knew is suddenly scripted in neon.

This is the story of George, for whom it happened in reverse. In and out of trouble as a boy, there seemed to be no direction in his life. George the young man had no thoughts of becoming an actor. But the producers who discovered him recognized a natural talent. Somewhere, buried beneath all that toughness, there was a freewheeling style . . . a beguiling nonchalance that attracted people to him. This, decided the box-office barons, would make him a star.

George's first film was completed in record time. Only a few days covered the entire shooting. Everyone on the set was convinced, and the elated producers saw the character they had counted on come to life.

It was a dream, for a newcomer. Remember, George had never acted before. But his supporters had faith . . . so much, in fact, that he received twenty-five thousand dollars for his first job in the industry.

When young George got the check, what do you think he did? No, he didn't lose it all to slow horses and fast women. But neither did he put it in a bank. You see, those five figures on that little slip of paper symbolized his first success as an actor. Proudly, repeatedly, he displayed the check to all his friends and anyone else who might be impressed along the way. Carried it with him wherever he went.

Months passed. For George and his check, the honeymoon had come to an end. By the time he finally got it to the bank, much had happened. The motion picture, already released, had failed. The producers were bankrupt. The check . . . bounced. All George had to show for his hour of glory was an ego as deflated as his pockets.

If the failure of his screen career was easier to take than you'd think, it was because he'd had his heart set on another from the very beginning. The silent-film producers who spotted George had him pegged as a star. And they were right. But it would take many years, many failures, and another profession to prove it.

George would act again. In a successful film. But only after he'd made a fabulous name for himself elsewhere. In that circuitous route to stardom, he would bring to the screen his own character and all the characteristics his fans had come to love.

George never shook the toughness of youth, and that rugged, blunt-faced determination is summed up in a nickname the world knows well. If companion meteors have since flared out and burned to cosmic dust, his star still shines and always will. . . .

George Herman "Babe" Ruth.

Charlie Ross was the teacher's pet. High school graduating class
1901.

The teacher was Miss Tillie Brown. An English teacher. Young.
Attractive.

Everyone knew Charlie was Miss Brown's favorite . . . and because Miss Brown was such a popular teacher, it placed a lot of
pressure on Charlie.

Charlie had to work very hard to defend his title "teacher's
pet." He had to read and to study a little bit more than everyone
else. Even at that, the other students made jokes behind Charlie's
back. Charlie had better amount to something someday, they said,
or Miss Brown would never forgive him.

As you have guessed, Charlie did amount to something one day
. . . and perhaps, directly because of what happened during graduation exercises.

Addresses had been made. Diplomas had been handed out. And
something else no one had expected.

When Charlie Ross's turn came to receive his diploma, Miss
Tillie Brown . . . the beloved English teacher . . . rose to con-
gratulate Charlie personally . . . with a kiss!

That did it.

Charlie may have been class valedictorian; he may have been

editor of the student yearbook; he may even have been the teacher's pet. Did that entitle him to such an honor, a kiss from the class's cherished Miss Brown?

After graduation exercises were over, there should have been laughing, shouting, excitement.

Instead, there was quiet disappointment.

Many of the graduates, especially the boys, resented Miss Brown's unabashed display of favoritism. So much so that a handful of them approached Miss Brown, and one of them asked her why others had been so conspicuously neglected.

Miss Brown stood firm. She said Charlie had earned the special recognition. She said when the others had done something worthwhile, they'd get kissed, too. She'd see to it.

If this made the other boys feel a little better, it made Charlie Ross feel worse.

He had been the object of this minor scandal. He had been the cause of all those hurt feelings. In life after high school, Charlie would most certainly have to prove himself worthy of Miss Brown's congratulatory kiss.

And he did.

In the years that followed, Charlie worked very hard. He entered the newspaper business and eventually so distinguished himself that he was hand-picked by President Harry Truman to be White House press secretary.

Now, the selection of Charlie Ross for the job was no mere accident. The leader of the boys who approached Miss Brown for the graduating class of 1901, the one who told her that he and the others felt left out, was Harry Truman himself.

And it was to him that she had said, "Do something worthwhile and you'll get your kiss."

Is it any wonder that Charlie Ross's first duty as presidential press secretary, his very first assignment, was to call Miss Tillie Brown in Independence, Missouri?

The message Ross delivered from the President of the United States: "How about that kiss I never got? Have I done something worthwhile enough to rate it now?"

He got his kiss. That is THE REST OF THE STORY.

He is lying there in the grass, hiding and thinking.

He has studied the little girl's habits. He knew she would come outside her grandfather's house midafternoon to play.

He hated himself for this.

In his whole miserable, messed-up life he'd never considered anything so callous as kidnaping.

Yet here he was, lying in the grass, hidden by trees from the house, waiting for an innocent, red-haired, two-year-old girl child to come within reach.

It was a long wait; there was time to think.

Maybe all his life Harlan had been in too much of a hurry.

He was five when his Hoosier farmer daddy had died.

At fourteen he dropped out of Greenwood School and hit the road.

He tried odd jobs as a farm hand, hated it.

Tried being a streetcar conductor and hated that.

At sixteen he lied about his age and joined the Army—and hated that, too. When his one-year enlistment was up he headed for Alabama, tried blacksmithing and failed.

He became a railroad locomotive fireman with the Southern Railroad. He liked that. Figured maybe he had found himself.

At eighteen he got married, and within months, wouldn't you

know she announced she was pregnant the day he announced he'd been fired again?

Then, one day, while he was out job hunting, his young wife gave away all their possessions and went home to her parents.

Then came the depression.

Harlan couldn't win for losing, as they say.

He really tried.

Once, while working at a succession of railroad jobs, he tried studying law by correspondence.

But he dropped out of that, too.

He tried selling insurance, selling tires.

He tried running a ferryboat, running a filling station. No use.

Face it—Harlan was a loser.

And now here he was hiding in the weeds outside Roanoke, Virginia, plotting a kidnaping.

As I say, he'd watched the little girl's habits, knew about her afternoon playtime.

But, this one day, she did not come out to play, so his chain of failures remained unbroken.

Late in life he became chief cook and bottle washer at a restaurant in Corbin. And did all right until the new highway bypassed the restaurant.

And then his expected life span ran out.

He's not the first man nor will he be the last to arrive at the twilight of life with nothing to show for it.

The bluebird of happiness, or whatever, had always fluttered just out of reach.

He'd stayed honest—except for that one time when he had attempted kidnaping. In fairness to his name it must be noted that it was his own daughter he'd meant to kidnap from his runaway wife.

And they both returned to him, the next day, anyway.

But now the years had slid by and a lifetime was gone and he and they had nothing.

He had not really felt old until that day the postman brought his first Social Security check. That day, something within Harlan resented, resisted, and exploded.

The Government was feeling sorry for him.

You had all those hitless times at bat, the Government was saying, you've had it.

It's time to give up and retire.

His restaurant customers in Corbin said they'd miss him, but his Government said sixty-five candles on the birthday cake is enough. They sent him a pension check and told him he was "old."

He said, "Nuts."

And he got so angry he took that $105 check and started a new business.

Today that business is prospering and so, at age eighty-six, is he.

For the man who failed at everything save one thing . . . the man who might have been a law-breaking kidnaper had he not also failed at that . . . the man who never got started until it was time to stop . . . was Harland Sanders. Colonel Harland Sanders.

The new business he started with his first Social Security check . . . was Kentucky Fried Chicken. Now you know THE REST OF THE STORY.

55. BLACK BART'S THREAT

His name was Charles E. Boles.

You know him, history remembers him, as the California outlaw who terrorized Wells Fargo for more than seven years.

Black Bart.

By the second year of his infamous career, Black Bart was among the most frequently repeated names in the California newspapers. Feature writers glorified his daring, for Black Bart . . . worked alone!

When he was least expected, Bart would appear in the middle of a stagecoach trail, brandishing a double-barrel, twelve-gauge shotgun, his face concealed beneath a hood.

And though Bart was indeed a menacing figure, he was an amateur poet too! He usually left his incredulous victims with a few lines of original verse.

From the Sierra Nevada foothills to the Sonoma Coast of California was outlaw territory. But not even an outlaw could pass that way without thinking twice . . . about Black Bart.

During Bart's reign of terror, between 1875 and 1883, he is credited with twenty-nine stagecoach robberies. And so bold were those twenty-nine robberies that the lone, hooded bandit became the most celebrated desperado of his time.

His penchant for stagecoaches contracted by Wells Fargo led many to believe that Bart had a vendetta against the company.

While this might have been true, the romanticized fiction of Black Bart as a gallant hero fighting singlehandedly against a giant corporation became so popular that even some Wells Fargo officials started believing it.

As it turns out, the facts surrounding Black Bart's criminal career are more incongruous than the fantasies.

For example, Bart was finally caught not by a gunslinging sheriff or by an armed posse . . . but by a detective!

During Bart's last robbery, he was wounded, got away.

Afterward, while they were combing the hills for a trace of him, a bloodstained handkerchief was discovered. On this handkerchief, in one corner . . . F.X.O.7.

A laundry mark!

That's right, the telltale laundry mark on a piece of fine linen led to the arrest and conviction of California's most feared outlaw.

San Francisco supersleuth Harry Morse canvassed a hundred laundries and laundry agencies in that city before making the right connection. When he did . . . when Detective Morse found the right establishment, who was there to pick up his laundry? Black Bart himself!

Bart went into custody peaceably.

He returned the loot from his last heist, pleaded guilty to the robbery, received a light sentence. After four years serving as druggist for the prison doctor at San Quentin, he was back on the street. As far as anyone knows, Charles E. Boles . . . the original Black Bart . . . never committed another crime.

If you're wondering how the hooded, shotgun-wielding tyrant of the stagecoach trails got off with a virtual reprimand, you should know what the authorities discovered about Black Bart . . . when the hood came off.

Instead of a hard-riding equestrian, they found a man who was so frightened of horses, he traveled to and from all his robberies on foot.

Instead of a bloodthirsty young desperado from Death Valley, they found an aging gentleman from Decatur, Illinois . . . who never once in all his career as a bad man fired a shot . . . because he never once . . . loaded his gun!

And now you know THE REST OF THE STORY.

56. I AM MR. PIERCE

What you're about to hear is the profile of a hit-and-run. No morals. No conclusions. Just the facts.

Back in '53, a prominent attorney named Frank Pierce was driving home from a friend's house. It was late at night, but road conditions were normal.

At a downtown intersection a senior citizen, Mrs. Nathan Lewis, was crossing the street. She did not see Frank bearing down upon her, nor presumably did he see the aged woman in the middle of the road.

Within moments, Mrs. Lewis was hit, sprawled to the ground.

A nearby patrolman, officer Stanley Edelin, who had witnessed everything from a side street, took out after Frank and pulled him over.

No inebriation tests were administered, and Frank told Officer Edelin he had not intended to leave the scene of the accident.

By some miracle, Mrs. Lewis escaped with minor cuts and bruises. She would be all right.

Frank was taken to headquarters. Reckless driving. Possible hit-and-run.

According to the police blotter, Frank's only words during the interrogation were, "I am Mr. Pierce."

A needless accident. An almost-tragedy.

Why? That is THE REST OF THE STORY. . . .

In relating the events leading up to Frank's hit-and-run, I'm not attempting to excuse him but to explain him.

In the months preceding, there was already trouble at home. The forty-eight-year-old lawyer was in the process of relocating his practice, moving South. His wife, a fragile, nervous woman, had begun to panic at the thought of abandoning the cooler climate, which she preferred.

A basically jovial, even-tempered man, Frank was a stunning contrast to his wife, Jane.

Jane was a devoutly religious woman who, during their nineteen years of marriage, regarded her husband's increasing success with skepticism.

Every time Frank had a drink, Jane cringed. Frank drank more.

Around that period of transition when Frank was changing jobs, he took Jane and their only son, aged nine, on a train from Boston to Concord, New Hampshire.

On that journey, the train derailed, crashed. Both parents were unhurt. Their nine-year-old son . . . crushed to death.

Suffering greatly at the loss, Jane became chronically ill, took to her bed. Superficially she resigned herself to the tragedy's having been God's will, while surreptitiously relating it to the abandonment of Frank's first practice.

It was at that time that Frank, guilt-ridden, adopted the habit of driving around late at night to relax, to think. Perhaps . . . to drink.

Although there is no hard evidence that Frank was either morose or intoxicated the night he left a friend's house on the southeastern side of the city and ran down an old woman in the middle of the street, it is at least possible. Perhaps probable.

And if there are any axioms that might be attached to this story, they're old ones: If you're unhappy, don't spread it. If you drink, don't drive.

Frank was lucky. The woman he hit was not seriously hurt. All charges were dropped.

Oh, did I mention that Frank was driving . . . a one-horse shay . . . in 1853?

If he got off light, it was perhaps because his dad was a former state governor.

Or perhaps because he . . . Frank Pierce . . . Franklin Pierce . . . was then President of the United States!

57. THE STING

Not many years ago, the ultimate put-down was "plastic." College-agers clamored about "plastic people," and homeowners moaned over "plastic paneling." If it was plastic, it wasn't real. It's taken us a while, but we're all coming to know just how real plastic can be. The handsome, superhard finishes . . . the once breakable now unbreakable.

The industry itself would never have been born were it not for the myriad shortages that demanded it. Frequently, lack of something leads to something else more important than the original.

It was ever true.

There was a fabric shortage in the eighteenth century. And in the process of resolving that need, the whole world was changed.

René Antoine Ferchault de Réaumur. You may or may not have heard of him. He was one of those fellows whose discoveries and accomplishments meant more to fellow scientists than to ordinary folks. For example, he invented a thermometer that's still used in biochemistry experiments. Few of us have ever seen one.

The son of a judge, Réaumur's first intentions were to study law. After two years in law school, he became interested in the sciences. There was no time to lose, so he grounded himself thoroughly in mathematics, physics, chemistry . . . prepared himself for further study in Paris.

All this took place in one year. When he was twenty. Five years later, Réaumur was admitted to the French Academy of Sciences as a result of his outstanding work in mathematics.

But Réaumur's first love, as it turns out, was natural science. Nature. Birds and insects especially fascinated him. And it was that fascination which would eventually, indirectly, alleviate the fabric shortage of his day. Here's THE REST OF THE STORY.

Réaumur's favorite recreation was to hike through the forest. Not only did this afford him the time to ponder certain scientific problems, but it gave him the opportunity to observe nature firsthand.

He was out on one of his woodland walks when he discovered the handiwork of a particular insect. Marveling at the substance it had produced, he took a sample and hurried home to study it. Months went by and friends began to ask, "Where's Réaumur?" Well, he was doing a bit of scientific detective work.

Finally, in November of the year, he addressed the French Academy. He told them that the linen shortage was a thing of the past and at last the future was here. He was right.

That was 1719.

Today, the industry that grew out of Réaumur's accidental discovery has grown into a fourteen-billion-dollar one. Hardly a single aspect of modern life would be the same without it. And yet it has little to do with linen.

Cloth was used for more than clothes, two and a half centuries ago. It was used to produce something else that Réaumur's insects had been making all along.

The scientist's forest find . . . was an abandoned wasp's nest. They shared their secret with him, and he with us.

For yesterday's man used skin and leaves and rags.

Wasps use wood . . . to make paper.

If you looked around long enough, you'd probably find "I love Lucy" scrawled on some national monument in Washington, D.C.

And it would be testimony to one of the most ravishing and popular bachelorettes in the history of our nation's capitol.

Now, this dates back a long time before Fanne Foxe and Elizabeth Ray . . . and by drawing the correlation I don't mean to imply that Lucy's morals were questionable.

But she *was* ravishing and she *was* popular and just about any young bachelor who *was* anybody was probably in love with Lucy.

Lucy Lambert Hale. She was the younger daughter of John P. Hale, one of New Hampshire's Civil War senators.

When she was only twelve, a Harvard freshman named Will Chandler was sending her love poems. Lucy was quite fond of the young man, but she was only twelve and it didn't get much further than correspondence. It's a matter of coincidence that young Will grew up to become Secretary of the Navy and, finally, a United States senator from New Hampshire.

Maybe it was partly a coincidence. You see, lovely Lucy Hale seemed to attract the more noteworthy gentlemen of Washington, especially when they were yet to become noteworthy. Lucy could "pick a star," you might say.

Lucy Hale was sixteen when she met Oliver. He was two years older than she . . . but still no match!

Like Will Chandler, Oliver was a Harvard student. He met Lucy while vacationing in Maine and began writing her love letters as soon as he returned to Cambridge. She changed schools from Hanover, in New Hampshire, to a boarding school in Boston, presumably to be closer to Oliver . . . but at the same time she was moving closer to the entire Harvard University. It would seem that the competition was too much for Oliver, and so, instead of devoting his life to the lovely Lucy Hale, he went on to become the man you know as Justice Oliver Wendell Holmes.

There is another man on the list of Lucy's luminary lovers, another beau in her bouquet. Perhaps, through him, some additional light might be shed on a time-worn topic.

This fellow was far and away her most experienced suitor. His name was John, and he was a known "ladies' man." That's probably why he chose to remain unknown during their first acquaintance.

John sent Lucy a letter, right out of the blue, on Valentine's Day of 1862:

My Dear Miss Hale

Were it not for the License which a time-honored observance of this day allows, I had not written you this poor note. . . .

You resemble in a most remarkable degree a lady, very dear to me, now dead and your close resemblance to her surprised me the first time I saw you.

This must be my apology for any apparent rudeness noticeable.—To see you has indeed afforded me a melancholy pleasure, if you can conceive of such, and should we never meet nor I see you again—believe me, I shall always associate you in my memory, with her, who was very beautiful, and whose face, like your own I trust, was a faithful index of gentleness and amiability.

With a Thousand kind wishes for your future happiness I am, to you—

A Stranger

Of course, John made certain that Lucy could easily discover his identity . . . and she did discover it . . . and they got together . . . and they became engaged. Did that result in THE REST OF THE STORY?

Just as this was Lucy's heretofore most serious involvement, there is every indication that it was John's too! John the "ladies' man" . . . a mere lad of twenty-four and already sought after, already enormously popular himself . . . lady-killer John had been captivated and captured by barely-twenty-year-old Lucy Hale.

When he fell, he fell hard! There were many jealousies in that long courtship. The lovers were still quarreling in the spring of 1865. They quarreled through President Lincoln's second inaugural address, the tickets to which Lucy had obtained from her senator father. They quarreled the night after John discovered Lucy dancing with Robert Lincoln, the President's eldest son, at the National Hotel in Washington.

I've made reference to the Lincoln family for a couple of reasons. In the first place, it helps to keep the dates straight in our minds. And in the second place, President Lincoln had recently appointed Lucy's father ambassador to Spain. Lucy was getting ready to go with him.

What I'm trying to say is that John had a number of good reasons to hold a grudge against the Lincolns. And though I'm not saying that those reasons might justify or even explain what John did shortly thereafter, they could serve as a clue or a key to unlock an already twisted mind.

For Lucy there was a happy ending. She eventually married Will Chandler, the Harvard-man-turned-senator who sent her love poems when she was twelve.

But it would be many years before she could forget her first fiancé . . . the dashing young actor . . . the lady-killer no one but Lucy could tame . . . and perhaps not even she.

John Wilkes Booth.

59. GENTLE JOHN HENRY

Gentle John Henry was born in Griffin, Georgia, the son of a Confederate Army major.

As a boy, John was taught proper bearing and courtly manners, befitting his prestigious family. But one thing disturbed his daddy: John could not hold his own in a fight.

Fully grown in his late teens, John stood five ten, was painfully thin . . . and was tortured by his fear of physical violence.

One day, the violence was unavoidable.

He was roughed up by a ruffian over the right to use a swimming hole. John's father promptly sent him to Baltimore, to advance the boy's education in a less threatening environment. He was enrolled in the Baltimore Dental College.

John was entirely agreeable. With the home-town bullies at a safe distance, he studied diligently for two years and completed the course in dentistry. Then he moved to Atlanta, Georgia, where he would begin his postgraduate practice.

For a while, John worked alongside one of the most prominent dentists in that city, frequently taking over his elder colleague's practice.

Eventually homesickness set in and John, now twenty-two, returned to Griffin to establish himself there.

It was a comfortable little offce, at the southwestern corner of Solomon and State. And though John's life appeared to be complete, there was another personal concern which had been haunting him. Tuberculosis.

The already gentle young man became even more subdued as the worry over his health increased. One day, a quaking, wan John Henry sat in the office of his general practitioner and was told he was going to die.

John asked how long he had to live.

The physician's gaze fell. He was quiet for a moment. "Perhaps a drier climate might add a year or two." And that was all he said.

So it seemed that gentle John Henry . . . the boy who couldn't hold his own in a fight . . . the retiring young man who had fled violence to become a dentist . . . had returned home to a battle he could not win.

But, just this once in his brief, unassuming, mild-mannered life, John Henry wanted to fight back!

How could he die if he had not yet lived?

Next day, John packed his bags and his dental instruments. If even a few precious hours could be gained in a drier climate, then that's where John would go.

First stop, Dallas . . . on a one-way trip to immortality.

It was a Dallas cowpoke dental patient who first met the new John Henry. The cowboy complained about his treatment, the ensuing argument escalated, the dentist pulled out a .45 . . . and blew the cowboy clean away.

The frustration of a waning, yet-to-be-experienced life carved for the notorious itinerant Wild West gambler thirty notches on his gun. John Henry would one day die of the respiratory disease that plagued him. It was not a year . . . or two . . . but fourteen years later! And in those fourteen years, John bet and blazed and blasted his way into the pages of western history.

John Henry was once described as "the nerviest, speediest, deadliest man with a six-gun I ever saw!" This unequivocal praise . . . came from Marshal Wyatt Earp.

Perhaps by now you've guessed that John Henry . . . the boy who couldn't hold his own in a fight . . . the mild-mannered dentist who found life only after facing death . . . the much-feared, drinking, gambling, gun-slinging friend of Wyatt Earp . . . was John Henry "Doc" Holliday!

And now you know THE REST OF THE STORY.

60. AN AFFAIR OF THE HEART

In an up-tempo era of constant medical advancement, there's good news tonight. . . .

There are two related items . . . the first, dated April:

> *A new centrifuge has been developed . . . a centrifuge capable of separating blood cells from blood plasma. More to follow.*

The second item has an even more recent dateline:

> *Research at Rockefeller Institute has culminated in the successful design of an artificial heart and lung . . . in which whole organs . . . animal or human . . . can be kept alive indefinitely. The organs may be preserved for study . . . or for use as chemical factories where vital substances might be produced. The supply of such substances would be practically unlimited.*

If these stories did not make headlines, there's a reason for it. The researcher . . . the inventor of the hemo-centrifuge and the designer of the artificial heart and lung . . . one and the same man . . . had been working in secret.

But who might he be? Barnard? DeBakey?

No, his name was Charles Augustus.

He finished the hemo-centrifuge in April . . . of 1932.

The design for the artificial heart and lung was complete in 1935. And though you say you've never heard of Charles Augustus, I'll bet you have.

He was born in Detroit on February 4, 1902.

As far as we know, he had no early ambition to be a medical researcher. But we do know that it was on his father's dairy farm that Charles came into contact with his first centrifuge . . . the cream separator. Whether the cream separator was Charles's earliest model for the hemo-centrifuge is not known. It seems reasonable.

Charles's father, ten years a U.S. congressman, knew the importance of a good education and wanted a solid base of knowledge for his son. So Charles went to college at the University of Wisconsin. It was there, after two years, that the young man decided what he would do with his life.

Charles's interest in the Rockefeller Institute began one day when a supply of pneumonia serum was flown from there to Quebec . . . to save the life of one of Charles's close friends. Two years later, he joined the staff at Rockefeller to begin his remarkable research . . . in secret.

This research eventually culminated in a book, coauthored by Dr. Alexis Carrel, *The Culture of Organs*. Although its contents are extremely valuable, Charles would have to wait another fifteen years for his well-earned Pulitzer prize . . . and that for another volume.

In the years before his death, Charles Augustus devoted himself to ecology. Again working for the betterment of mankind, quietly.

If you don't recognize the man about whom you've just heard, it is perhaps because he wanted it that way. For Charles Augustus has been described as the best-known, least-understood figure . . . in another field, unrelated to medicine. And that is THE REST OF THE STORY.

When the pneumonia serum had to be flown to the rescue of a friend he, Charles, flew it there.

But if his brush with medicine was an affair of the heart . . .

then it would have to be a secret affair . . . for that's the way he was. In fact, some called him . . . the Lone Eagle.

For the man who designed the artificial heart and lung would have to wait for his Pulitzer prize. The book for which *it* was awarded was *The Spirit of St. Louis* . . . by Charles Augustus Lindbergh.

61. CLARENCE WHO?

Today, in an age of nostalgia, in an age of vicariousness . . . at a time of twice-removed excitement and secondhand adventure . . . some content themselves with retracing the steps of the early explorers, the pioneers, and the pilgrims. It's still dangerous.

Perhaps the Kon Tiki raft was in the vanguard of this movement. Later, others would attempt to ford Bering Strait in a kayak . . . to struggle across the Pacific in a sampan or an outrigger canoe. And it's still exciting enough so that some are willing to die trying.

One Irish author even attempted to prove that the Irish discovered America, by rowing his way here from there.

Now, with people crossing the ocean in hours, we've forgotten the thrill of what Lindbergh really did in a highly fallible, one-lung light plane. It just isn't done . . . even today . . . crossing oceans non-stop in a single-engine aircraft. But even after Lindy, many have dreamed of reliving his triumph, his accomplishment.

Now let me tell you about Clarence. Clarence Chamberlin. He, too, was fascinated with the idea of crossing the Atlantic solo.

And some might say that with the Lone Eagle to show the way . . . that after Lindbergh proved it could be done, the flight would be an easy one.

But that wasn't the case.

Pilot Clarence Chamberlin must have admired Lucky Lindy. The plane Chamberlin chose was so similar. The engine, almost identical.

Perhaps, in the same way modern-day Olympians take pride in besting past records set, Clarence would go one up on Lindbergh: He'd take off from New York all right . . . but he wouldn't stop till he got to Berlin.

There was a good deal of excitement connected with his flight plan. Movie rights were already being discussed long before Chamberlin ever left the ground. There was even a discussion as to whether Clarence himself was right for the adventure, because he wasn't the "motion picture type."

Before long, a millionaire named Levine put up the money, a designer named Bellanca drew up the plans, and an aircraft called the *Columbia* was ready to skim the Atlantic.

Chamberlin got his first good-weather map on Friday afternoon, June 3, but last-minute check was still running and he wouldn't take off till Saturday morning.

There were thirteen 5-gallon tins of gasoline aboard, each to be emptied into the main tank as the flight progressed and then thrown into the sea.

Keeping the weight down was important, but other necessities included a pistol for firing distress signals, a rubber lifeboat, a flashlight, two vacuum bottles filled respectively with chicken soup and coffee, ten chicken sandwiches, a half dozen oranges, two canteens of water, some army emergency rations, some chewing gum, and extra flight clothes for use at night over the North Atlantic.

Chamberlin worked on his plane in the hangar until 1:30 Saturday morning. He was back in his hotel-room bed at 2:00 . . . left a wake-up call for 3:30 . . . didn't sleep. Had he forgotten anything? Would the good weather hold for the morning? How might Lindbergh have felt, he wondered, just hours before *his* daring flight?

At any rate, a few minutes after 6:00 A.M. Clarence was up and on his way to reliving history. And he made it . . . across the Atlantic . . . past Paris . . . and on to Berlin . . . to better Lindbergh's record.

That you've probably not heard of Clarence Chamberlin can be attributed to the fact that his feat had been previously accomplished. That does not diminish what he did. It was still daring, still dangerous . . . and especially when you consider one other factor.

Had Clarence Chamberlin been first he'd have been famous. But he wasn't first.

His name . . . and the nostalgic flight he took . . . received comparatively little attention only because another pilot, Slim Lindbergh, had made a lesser flight . . .

Just fourteen *days* before.

62. AN ANTHEM FOR THE ENEMY

War song.

The two words themselves are somewhat in conflict with each other. And yet, for the sake of world culture, this is a type of music of stirring importance. Remember, our own national anthem is a war song of sorts.

Anthropologists theorize that this was among the first music to be sung. Primitive people probably conjured their cult rituals with the war song . . . used it to accompany fiery dancing.

In ancient Greece, the songs of Tyrtaeus were sung by Spartan warriors at their campfires. Still other songs were used to harden the spirits of those about to enter battle.

The words to many anthems of war are based on sound psychological principles. What could be more encouraging than the brave deeds of forefathers or a victory projected, predicted, in music?

By the end of the fifteenth century, army units began to have trumpeters, drummers, pipers attached to them. Their music supported the discipline of marching . . . the urge to battle.

It was so in the American Revolution.

You know the songs we sang. But now you're going to hear about an enemy anthem . . . a rhyme for the Redcoats.

Some say this British tune in two/four can be traced to a song of French vineyard workers. Others argue that it came from a Spanish sword dance or a German harvest tune or a Dutch peasant song.

We're just not sure.

But we do know that British soldiers sang it during the French and Indian War . . . a full two decades before the signing of the Declaration of Independence. And they would use it to shatter the courage of the colonists throughout the Revolution, sometimes posting troops to sing it outside a church during colonial religious services. It was meant to taunt us, to make us afraid.

Then a curious thing happened to this demoralizing melody. We stole it. Just lifted it, words and all, from the voices of our enemies.

One patriot suggested that we should change the words, befitting the colonial cause. Although he, a man named Francis Hopkinson, successfully came up with a new set of lyrics, our forefathers favored the original. Oh, Hopkinson's "Battle of the Kegs" was sung, all right. But we, perpetuating a long tradition of musical psychological warfare, knew what hurt the most. So the enemy heard their own song, their own words, thrown right back in their ears.

And it worked.

It became a favorite in every camp. It was heard in battle, in defeat, in victory. It was even played at the final surrender of General Cornwallis.

Yes, the enemy anthem worked for the Americans during the Revolutionary War. Such was its subsequent popularity that it brilliantly survived the war itself. Benjamin Carr used it in an orchestral medley, the *Federal Overture*, written in 1794. A century later, visiting European composers would write variations on the tune, honoring the Americans and their efforts during the Revolution.

This song was intended to needle American troops during our Revolution . . . until with incomparable American mischief we turned the needle around and *they* got the point.

The Redcoat rhyme that we made our own forevermore . . . was "Yankee Doodle"!

63. THE VIOLINIST WHO NEARLY BECAME
PRESIDENT OF ISRAEL

Christmas Eve in Princeton, New Jersey, usually fulfills the picture-postcard promise of Christmas.

And it was so, on that one particular Christmas Eve, long ago.

Church bells pealed in the distance. A light snowfall kissed the quaint Princeton houses, and door-to-door carol singers made their way . . . to one particular door.

The violinist's home.

The gentle violinist.

"O little town of Bethlehem," the boys sang, "how still we see thee lie. . . ."

In moments the door opened . . . and the gentle old violinist stood in the doorway to greet the carolers.

"Above thy deep and dreamless sleep, the silent stars go by. . . ."

The musician turned away . . . turned back into the house. Shortly he reappeared . . . with his violin!

There he completed a picture too intimate for a postcard . . . a sound too inspiring for any but this story.

The great man . . . the gentle old musician . . . accompanied the midnight carolers on his beloved instrument through each verse of the age-old hymn.

Then, without a word to break the spell, the young people

turned away silently and the old man slowly closed the door. At once there was only the distant pealing of the bells, and the snowfall.

And if this true story . . . this real-life scene from a year long past . . . if it is made more wonderful, it is not because a seasoned violin was brought out of retirement for one last spontaneous recital, but because the violinist himself had the best reason of all *not* to celebrate that snowy Christmas scene.

The great genius was a Jew, and so revered was he that the very presidency of Israel once could have been his.

But here is THE REST OF THE STORY. . . .

Musicians will tell you, every great genius has his idol. This violinist's idol was Mozart.

In his own words, the musician described the turning point in his early musical career: "I really began to learn only when I was about thirteen years old . . . mainly, after I had fallen in love with Mozart's sonatas. The attempt to reproduce their singular grace compelled me to improve my technique. I believe, on the whole, that love is a better teacher than sense of duty . . . with me, at least, it certainly was."

Once, a friend asked the violinist to comment on modern times. When the musician was a boy, wars were fought with rifles and cannons. Now the entire world might be devastated. What did that mean to the old man?

The violinist hesitated, sat back thoughtfully in his chair.

"It would mean," he said at last, "that people would no longer hear Mozart."

For him, this most deeply conveyed the end of civilization.

On many an occasion, he would break an hours-long chamber music session with the same observation.

Mozart's music was so pure that it seemed to have been ever-present in the universe, waiting to be discovered by the master.

So the great genius had an idol . . . and that idol was Mozart. For him, Mozart was what the world was all about.

And when this violinist was offered the highest Jewish honor . . . the presidency of Israel . . . he declined, saying that he felt unqualified for a role that involved human relations.

Yet who could have felt human warmth more deeply than the

musician who worshiped Mozart, than the old Jewish gentleman who serenaded Christian carolers from his last home?

For him, Mozart was not a composer but a discoverer, a discoverer of celestial music that lay waiting in the universe.

So when the violinist began to explore the universe, those closest to him believed that he was merely searching . . . for what Mozart had found.

More logically this musician's idol might well have been Sir Isaac Newton, but he counted himself first as a violinist.

For the musician who worshiped Mozart . . . the revered genius who could have been president of Israel . . . was the man who literally altered the meaning of infinity, hoping to discover . . . music.

He was Dr. Albert Einstein.

Nearly a hundred years before Freud or Tennessee Williams might have raised your eyebrow, John and Bob . . . were inseparable.

From the day they met, they so enjoyed each other's company that they ate from the same table, lived in the same house, slept in the same room.

In public they were never apart. In the privacy of their home, they greeted guests together. They were inseparable.

I don't know how you feel about this so far, but try to put yourself in Bob's place . . . when John died.

Theirs had been a constant companionship shared by few people on earth . . . few brothers . . . few husbands and wives. Now it was over.

A poet said of death, "Now, at last, for the first time you have given me pain." And so . . . for Bob.

John Gray was buried in the Greyfriars churchyard, Edinburgh, on a dismal spring morning in 1858.

Throughout his illness, Bob had never left his side. Afterward, at the funeral, Bob wept unashamedly. He watched wet-eyed and heartbroken as his friend was lowered into the ground.

When the ritual was finished, the minister and the attendants slowly left the churchyard, leaving Bob to his quiet grief. The story would have ended there had Bob's courage been greater or his sorrow less.

Instead, acquaintances passing Greyfriars later that evening found Bob still at the graveside, head bowed, silent. Remembering the kind attention John and Bob had shown them, "Come home with us," they said.

And Bob went home with them. But he would not stay.

Next morning, it was apparent his bed had not been slept in; Bob had gone back to the grave of his friend.

Many times he was gently urged from the churchyard. As many times, he returned to mourn.

It was for his own good that he leave, they said. But the reasoning was useless.

Bob never again saw the house he had shared with John.

Each day, Bob maintained his graveside vigil, and eventually the sexton at Greyfriars gave him official permission to stay.

In all Edinburgh this was an unprecedented display of grief, and the curious citizens frequently passed by to watch.

The neighborhood children . . . impressed . . . sometimes brought food and drink. Bob, though grateful, remained.

In inclement weather, a woman might bring him a shawl and a kind word or two. Once, a baroness was so deeply touched that she commissioned a bronze medal for him to wear. But Bob stayed . . . and everyone understood. For fourteen years.

For fourteen years Bob quietly kept his daily vigil. Then, one cold January morning in 1872, he was found at the graveside still, lifeless, his visage filled with a strange contentment.

Bob was buried nearby, to keep company in death the man he would not abandon in life.

Today, in front of the Candlemakers' Hall in Edinburgh, there is a fountain dedicated to the memory of Bob.

His friend, John Gray, who otherwise would have been forgotten, is remembered also because Bob . . . a little ruffle-coated Skye terrier . . . loved him. That is THE REST OF THE STORY.

65. THE TERRORIST

William was a political terrorist and jailbird . . . and the governor of New Jersey. And all within the space of four years.

But not in that order.

How did William, governor of New Jersey, go so far downhill so fast? The descent is even more remarkable when you consider the strength of his beginnings.

William was born to a rather distinguished and well-known father.

He was once postmaster of Philadelphia and served as clerk of the Pennyslvania Provincial Assembly.

A captain in the Army, his war record was excellent.

Through his father, William became acquainted with the higher-ups who helped him become governor of New Jersey.

And William was an enormously popular governor for quite some while, perhaps through the power of his own personality or perhaps through the previous popularity of his father's name. There's just no way to tell. All we know for certain is that the good times didn't last. Arguments with the legislature got William deeper and deeper into trouble until he was repudiated by the New Jersey Congress, declared dangerous, and imprisoned. Within two years, he'd be out of jail; in another two years, William would seek his revenge as leader of a terrorist army.

Now we're going to stop right here for a moment. This is not a tale of contemporary corruption. In fact, William was born in 1731 and it was not *his* political ideals that changed. It was the people of New Jersey who changed, caught in the shifting tide.

This was that agonizing hour in our nation's history when some American colonists wanted to break away from England—others did not. They remained loyal to the crown. William was a loyalist, a royalist, a monarchist. So this is really the story of how bitterness grew to hatred for an otherwise peaceful man.

In 1778, William was released from custody in exchange for some revolutionary prisoners. At that time, he fled to the safety of British-held New York. It was there, in New York, that the loyalists had been organizing themselves into small guerrilla bands. During the two years William had been imprisoned, the loyalists, calling themselves the "Refugees," had been launching infrequent small-scale attacks on New Jersey's patriot towns, using New York as a base of operations.

That is how William, the former governor of New Jersey, became involved in terrorist activity against the very state he had previously governed. But the dilemma did not end there.

For William, it was not enough to become merely involved. So when King George created an official Refugee Army in 1780, who was its leader? That's right. William. And now the attacks on New Jersey were neither small-scale nor infrequent.

Soon horror stories of arson, rape, mutilation, and murder spilled over the New Jersey landscape. Ex-Governor William was on the rampage. Retaliation followed. What had begun as military raids degenerated into personal vendettas on both sides. One historian described it as the "cruelest kind of warfare," those back-and-forth skirmishes between the Refugees and the New Jersey militia. In fact, the fighting was so bitter, so personal, that the ill feelings did not fade with the British capitulation at Yorktown in 1781. In 1782, the violence and brutality were still going on.

Revolutionary "Renaissance man" Benjamin Franklin made an interesting observation when he described the Revolution as a "civil war." It really was, you know. Even though the Declaration of Independence suggests that a united people opposed the British, nothing could have been further from the truth. It has never been accurately determined whether the loyalists or the patriots were in the majority when the Declaration was signed.

So Ben Franklin was right. The Revolution was really a civil war. How keenly that point is brought home in the story of New Jersey's governor-turned-terrorist, William . . . Franklin.

Ben Franklin's only son!

66. STRANGER ON THE ROAD

If Columbus actually stumbled over America on his way to India, then the term "discovery" is misleading. It is in many cases.

If the stories are true, a great scientific principle hit Sir Isaac Newton over the head . . . literally lifted Archimedes out of his bath. "I have found it!" he proclaimed . . . when, in fact, it had found him.

These are the strangers on the road. The answers that seek out the askers. The unexpected destinations on the way to somewhere else.

Our earliest discoveries were doubtless strangers on the road to nowhere. At least it's safe to assume, as anthropologists suggest, that primitive man did not go out looking for fire . . . did not set out to invent the wheel.

Many of our most recent discoveries were by-products of unrelated endeavor.

You might say that penicillin discovered British bacteriologist Alexander Fleming in 1928. So it was, a few short years before, that something else discovered Bill.

Bill was a tinkerer with lots of credentials. He received his technical training at a number of universities, including Cornell. He'd even been an associate of Thomas Edison for several years. But

Bill was an independent at heart, and finally his dream of independence came true.

He was an impressive man . . . tall, handsome, articulate, and with a reputable background to match. If he was a bit forgetful at times, there was much that made up for it.

In the early 1920s, Bill was working just outside Laurel, Mississippi. Back then, lumber mills used to burn scrap wood, and the mills near Laurel were no exception. It bothered Bill to see all that raw material going up in smoke, so he decided to do something with it . . . anything.

One experiment followed the next until Bill finally came up with a contraption that could blow up wood. That's right, just explode it into a fluffy, fibrous substance.

The device was quite simple, actually . . . a sealed container filled with wood chips. But when the container was heated and the increased pressure inside was released suddenly, the wood chips practically disintegrated.

Good insulation material, thought Bill. But the companies that were producing insulation at the time had other raw-material sources. Even if they were to use the new invention, they didn't need it.

Many experiments later, fate shook Bill's hand. He had an old letter press with a leaky valve . . . almost an antique. Perhaps he could use it to compress this wood fluff into mats. Then, at least, it would be easier to handle.

After repeating the process several times, Bill broke for lunch . . . forgetting to release the press. When he returned, he discovered that what ought to have been sheet insulation had been transformed into something else.

That was 1924. Bill was forty-seven back then. The company named for him would some day produce enough of that "something else" in a single year to make a four-foot-wide sidewalk that could circle the earth five and a half times. The world-wide industry he fathered remains a tribute . . . to his forgetfulness.

And the stranger he met in '24 is by no means a stranger any more. You may never have heard of William H. Mason. But now you'll remember THE REST OF THE STORY, the day he discovered . . . Masonite. Or was it the other way around?

67. REMEMBER THE "MAINE"?

Remember the *Maine?*

The *Maine* was the United States battleship that got us into the Spanish-American War. Not by the damage it did, but by the damage that was done to it. When the news screamed that a Spanish mine had sunk our ship in Havana Harbor, the now-famous war cry began that would hurl us into war with Spain:

"Remember the *Maine!*"

Her story is THE REST OF THE STORY. . . .

At 9:40 P.M. on February 15, 1898, the American battleship *Maine* exploded in the harbor of Havana, Cuba. There were 354 officers and men aboard; 266 lost their lives. The 300-foot vessel had been moored at the same spot since late January. Her purpose had been to defend American interests during the civil war that Cuba was fighting against Spain.

When news reached the mainland that a Spanish mine had dumped the *Maine* into Havana Harbor, the United States became actively involved. In six weeks, war was declared.

"Remember the *Maine!*" was the battle cry of that war. How dare they sink our ship! "Remember the *Maine!*" we cried as we went to war.

For data concerning the incident, we'll turn to Admiral H. G. Rickover and to representatives of the Taylor Naval Ship Research and Development Center and the Naval Surface Weapons Center.

Will you be patient with me while I delineate the findings of three separate examinations of the wreckage? It is important.

One examination was performed in connection with the 1898 United States court of inquiry.

A second was performed by Spanish divers, also in 1898.

And a third was performed in connection with the 1911 Board of Inspection and Survey.

The description of the wreckage contained in the 1898 Court of Inquiry report was obtained basically from diver inspections in muddy water. The Spanish divers who investigated the *Maine* the same year were even more handicapped, because they knew less about the ship's construction.

That brings us to 1911. The Board of Inspection and Survey report. The *Maine* had been submerged for thirteen years. And during those thirteen years, various salvage operations had been carried out. But when they inspected the ship in 1911, it would be in the open air.

A cofferdam was built.

The *Maine* was dewatered.

Every bit of the wreckage was accurately identified.

The displacements were measured.

And photographs were taken.

Despite the time lapse between the explosion and the 1911 inspection, contemporary studies by the Naval R & D Center and the Surface Weapons Center are based on the 1911 data.

These data, properly and carefully studied, are significantly revealing.

The statements in the 1911 report describing the wreckage . . . and the photographs and sketches of the wreckage . . . are generally consistent with one another.

The photographs were taken as the dewatering progressed and as the wreckage was dismantled.

In some cases, material was removed in the interval between pictures, and this was taken into account in the interpretation of the photographs.

I know it seems we're being careful, here, to document this most recent study of the *Maine*. But when you hear the conclusion of the report, you'll understand why it is important that we be certain.

This new revelation about our war with Spain may go mainly against the grain . . . but Admiral Rickover has confirmed his embarrassing theory with irrefutable fact.

For when experts now observe the photographs of the wreckage, with hull sides and whole deck structures peeled back, it leaves no doubt.

The explosion that sank our ship and catapulted us into the Spanish-American War was caused by a blast from twenty thousand pounds of powder . . . from the *inside*.

From as far back as anyone can remember, Kristoffer knew where he was going.

A clean-cut lad—bright, well behaved. The kind any parents would be proud to call their son.

His father, a major general in the Air Force, was immensely proud when young Kristoffer announced his intention someday to join the military. Kristoffer was ten, but even then—he knew what he must do.

First concern—grades, achievement. An air-tight academic record.

Then Brownsville, Texas-born Kristoffer was in high school. His dad was transferred to San Mateo, California. There were the usual family adjustments connected with the move. If ever a boy had the excuse to falter, it was then. Kristoffer . . . instead . . . excelled!

To his classmates, a square . . . remember that phrase? While the others bought be-bop records, Kristoffer bought ballads. When others stayed out late, Kristoffer stayed home, studied. He had a plan, and no one knew better than he what it would take.

After high school, Kristoffer attended private Pomona College, in Claremont, California. By this time, excellence was becoming an obsession. Scholastic excellence. Athletic excellence.

Kristoffer did not just play football . . . he had to be a football hero.

A Golden Gloves boxer.

A sports writer for the student paper.

An ROTC commander.

By now, any career in the world he might choose was drawing within his grasp. But not just any career for Kristoffer.

Before receiving his degree from Pomona, Kristoffer entered the *Atlantic Monthly* collegiate short-story contest . . . and won first prize. Then the ultimately prestigious academic recognition, a Rhodes scholarship and on to Oxford.

There was no hesitating . . . no soul-searching . . . no resting on his laurels. By the time Kristoffer reached Oxford, he had written one novel and was beginning a second. Book publishers were clamoring for his manuscripts, but Kristoffer had something else in mind. He'd told his daddy about it when he was ten. So after graduating from Oxford . . . after achieving as much as any young man could be expected to achieve, Kristoffer joined the Army.

He went through jump school.

Through Ranger school.

Through flight school.

He was a pilot, was a captain, was stationed in Germany, and at last, the big break. The assignment he had dreamed about. Back to the United States . . . to become a major . . . to become an instructor . . . at West Point.

Some just seem to know from the beginning where they're headed. What life expects of them. So it seemed to be . . . for Kristoffer. A boy who from the beginning of elementary school concerned himself with grades instead of grumbling. A boy who from the start was called a square . . . but didn't care. A football hero. A novelist. A Golden Gloves boxer. An ROTC commander. A Rhodes scholar. A young man like that . . . could go anywhere.

A captain about to become a major. A West Point instructor about to live a childhood dream. A young man like that . . . could go anywhere . . . could do anything . . . in or out of the military.

So Kristoffer . . . became a name you know.

He became the number-one recording artist of cow-country classics and hillbilly ballads, Kris Kristofferson.

Liberation!

The word alone carries with it a parenthetical exclamation point these days.

Its true definition is innocuous enough . . . even cheerful. But since the war-worn sixties spilled over into the corruption-torn seventies, few words have been capable of inspiring such a wide range of emotions.

Liberation!

In itself, a war cry. Why? Perhaps when you hear what I'm about to say, your perspective will readjust.

How long have "women's rights" been an issue. A century? Maybe. But "women's lib" and the overkill we sometimes associate with it are recent phenomena.

Originally, the very valid objective was equal pay for equal work.

Fine.

Then some were concerned about the survival of one's identity.

So far, so good.

But then, as is so frequently the case with an applause-thirsty cause, came the man haters and the bra burners . . . the little girls in Little League and all the rest.

Now some are saying they've gone too far. But wait till you hear how far they've gone.

I'm about to tell you *The Code of Love.*

This "code" was drafted by a group of women in May of seventy-four. Married women, mind you . . . all in the vanguard of the "lib" movement.

Their goal was to create, for themselves and for you, a new set of ethics . . . the guidelines for "liberated" conduct in modern times. In the process, they examined archaic standards and wound up with what amounts to a redefining of love itself.

In case it escaped your attention, this is *The Code of Love.* If you're at all sensitive or idealistic, or perhaps quite romantically inclined, read on anyway. . . .

"*Love cannot extend itself into marriage.* This is because lovers must grant everything to one another, mutually and gratuitously, without being constrained by any motive of necessity. Husband and wife, on the other hand, are bound by duty to deny each other nothing.

"Considering that no one should be deprived of love, *being married must not prevent one from seeking it elsewhere.* The only requirements of extramarital lovers are that they are honest, they are truly exciting and they have achieved adulthood. An insatiable appetite of one partner for the other is considered to be ideal.

"*No device is too extreme if it keeps this passion alive. Maintaining a secret affair may be favorable,* not so much for the sake of decency as for the sake of excitement. Whoever cannot keep a secret cannot love. Guarded jealousy may also be useful. And though we are not specifically recommending or even condoning the employment of force, *a resisting lover is always more desirable.*

"No one can be ultimately involved with two lovers at the same time. But just as nothing restricts one man from an affair with two women, *nothing prevents one woman from an affair with two men.*

"Love itself is always in a state of flux, either increasing or diminishing. After it begins to diminish, it dies rapidly. At that time, new love is an adequate excuse to quit the old.

"What one loses in sleep over love, one makes up for in what one does not eat. But persons who are either too wealthy or too happy in their own lives tend to lose the need of love. It should also serve as a warning that those who are prone to love are equally prone to fear."

I'm going to stop here.

What I've done is to paraphrase a rather lengthy thirty-one-point treatise and its concluding remarks. The collaborating women claim that polls were taken as advice for their new "code." They don't say whose.

Dr. Donald Jackson, founder and director of the Mental Research Institute, in Palo Alto, has his own ideas about *The Code of Love*. He concedes that the women who formulated it were intellectually and artistically superior to their husbands . . . and that they probably resented the inferior, nonproductive position into which they had been forced by a male-dominated society. Excessive leisure, says Dr. Jackson, doubtless afforded them the time to retaliate in this manner.

Now, in fairness to American women, let me say that *The Code of Love* was written in Europe.

And this panel of activists had never heard of "women's lib."

Actually they were a court of women led by the Countess of Champagne.

Their document is dated May 3 . . . A.D. 1174.

King Henry VIII, and Queen Catherine, and Anne Boleyn. A noted triangle in the romantic geometry of sixteenth-century England.

Anne began as an attendant to Queen Catherine, but quickly the two became rivals.

Eventually Anne won; she succeeded Catherine as Henry's queen.

But during that bitter, lopsided rivalry, the aging Queen Catherine . . . just once . . . got the upper hand.

Anne was only twelve when her father, Sir Thomas Boleyn, took her to France. There she entered the royal service, remained for three years. Even then her appearance was impressive though not particularly dazzling. She had large eyes, raven-black hair, a slender neck, and a soft, dark complexion. And she wore gloves. She wore gloves.

At fifteen, Anne returned to England. Her grandfather was one of King Henry's leading ministers, her father's prestige was ascending, and her elder sister was an attendant in the royal court. Quite naturally, Anne Boleyn herself became known and accepted in the court; soon she joined the queen's own entourage.

The poet Sir Thomas Wyatt was among her admirers at the time . . . and Henry Percy, heir to the earl of Northumberland.

But when talk of marriage started, rumors arose . . . something about sorcery.

And whispers said that that something related to those gloves.

At first King Henry was not attracted to Anne. Once, he'd even suggested her as a suitable wife for another earl.

But gradually, throughout Henry's increasing displeasure with Queen Catherine, the younger Anne Boleyn became his favorite. Then the subtle rivalry began.

In the midst of this competition with her youthful rival, the queen desperately mobilized her meager wit, her remaining authority, her sharp tongue.

These turned Henry more off than on. Also, Catherine had not given him a son. And as Henry's antipathy for the queen intensified, so did his desire for an heir to the throne, and so did his love for the lovelier Anne Boleyn.

The queen did not give up. And at times when the three were together, the queen would play her ace. "Why," she would ask, "would Anne not remove her gloves?"

And Anne, conspicuously hurt, would sit silent.

Catherine escalated her caustic taunt to open scorn. To the queen, Anne Boleyn epitomized her own waning youth. Her bitterness festered. She became increasingly petulant, overtly abusive: "Why would Anne not remove her gloves?" the queen demanded.

And Anne would respond only with silence. And eventually her patience was rewarded with a crown.

That Henry eventually turned against his younger bride with such vehemence that his anger cost her her life, may or may not have had anything to do with those gloves . . . with imagined sorcery . . . with what court tattlers called "the sign of a witch."

But history does record that, one desperate day, the older queen's taunt became an order. And that day, Catherine sought and got the upper hand if only for a little while.

For on that day, by royal command, Anne Boleyn removed her gloves . . . revealed for all and the king to see . . . the ugliness of a deformed left hand . . . the hand that had six fingers!

And now you know THE REST OF THE STORY.

71. THE PRODUCER

The reason for the success of many rock groups is no secret. For while their profligate polyphony in live performance is frequently drowned out by the cheering audience . . . it is their recordings that promote the concerts.

So the studio recording producer is the unsung superstar. It is he who must make sonic sense of an otherwise mess. It is he who must restore musical order, and in some cases he who must derive consistency . . . from nothing.

One brisk early spring, T. A. sat glumly in his New York recording studio, waiting for a piano player to show up.

As a record producer, T. A. was the top. A test recording in *his* studio with *his* engineers could make the best of even a poor performer. A contract with T. A.'s company might even mean overnight success.

Now, where was the piano player?

Presently, the studio door opened. A prominent nose with a lean, dour face attached to it peeked inside.

"Ah-hah!" cried T. A.

The slender musician timidly entered the studio, remained silent, fixing his gaze on the piano at the center of the room. Rapidly it became obvious that this musician was a foreigner . . . not only to the United States, but to recording studios.

The hesitation with which the piano player expressed himself in English was of no concern to producer T. A. It was music that T. A. was waiting for, and shortly the audition began.

Twenty bars into the session, T. A. threw up his hands. "Who told you you're a piano player?"

The engineers cringed, quietly shut down the equipment as T. A. continued, "You're a pounder, that's what you are . . . a pounder!"

No one said a word . . . least of all the slender, sad-looking musician who meekly rose from the bench, donned his overcoat and hat, and left.

Even for a proud musician of otherwise stunning confidence, this harsh criticism from producer T. A. had to hurt.

For T. A. was the best. His immaculate sense of balance, his taste, his discrimination, were legendary.

The records he produced were sure-fire winners, and apparently this lean, modest musician from across the ocean . . . had failed.

I should mention that T. A. and the piano player did eventually get together, although the producer never quite got used to the pounding.

Notes in T. A.'s log repeatedly recounted: "Something is the matter with this record" and "This tune unattractive."

But the piano player succeeded, nevertheless. His records sold . . . and we listen today with great awe to hear the music that bewildered the famous recording producer . . . the music of the incomparable Russian giant Sergei Rachmaninoff.

And T. A., the recording producer who never quite understood, the cranky old gentleman who was tops in his field . . . was practically the *only* man in his field, Thomas Alva Edison.

Although Edison's musical judgment was reverently trusted, though his comprehension of balance was considered impeccable . . . the great Rachmaninoff need not have taken the relentless criticism to heart.

Because Thomas Edison was a man more scientist than musician, a recording producer who was almost completely . . . deaf!

72.   JAMES

This is the ultimate success story.

It's about a boy, a boy named James, who entered the Army as a hospital assistant and wound up as Inspector General of the Army Medical Department.

This feat, remarkable in itself, is exaggerated by the outstanding surgical skill Dr. James Barry developed during his more than fifty years of service.

I'm sorry if you think the ending's been given away. But what made Dr. Barry ultimately successful is THE REST OF THE STORY.

On July 5, 1813, a scrawny eighteen-year-old lad banged on a United States Army registrar's door. His name was James Barry, he said, and he wanted to do hospital work.

"Hospital work, eh?" said the army official, smiling a bit. "And why do you wish specifically to do hospital work?"

The boy thought for a moment. "Because I love it!" he answered at last.

"And what is your experience in this field?" the army official wanted to know.

The boy stood in tense silence. It was then that the registrar really looked at him, observed the freckled face and the reddish hair.

"You're Scottish, aren't you?" asked the army official.

The boy's expression brightened. "Yes, sir!" he said enthusiastically. "In fact, my grandfather was a Scottish earl!"

True or not, the answer delighted the registrar, who was already impressed with the lad's eagerness to serve. He signed up young James, and so began one of the most incredible careers in the history of medicine.

Within a year and a half, James Barry, not yet twenty, rose to the title of assistant surgeon. You can imagine what he must have had to learn in those few months!

In another twelve years, Dr. Barry became surgeon major . . . and then deputy inspector general . . . and finally, after nearly a lifetime of devotion, James, the man who once stood as an inexperienced boy before an army registrar, became the Inspector General himself! The highest-ranking medical officer in the United States Army.

Notwithstanding his accumulation of stars and bars, there was another side to Dr. James Barry . . . a contradiction, you might say.

Once described as "the most skillful of physicians and the most wayward of men," this learned and fully competent doctor was also credited with an unusually quarrelsome temper. At least once that we know of, Dr. Barry, while stationed at the Cape of Good Hope, fought a duel. Throughout his army career James was often guilty of breaches of discipline, often sent home under arrest.

Now, you could write this off as the eccentricity of a medical genius; that's what headquarters did when confronted with Dr. Barry's offenses. May we suggest here that these somewhat regular outbursts of *macho* had another basis in an otherwise distinguished man?

You see, James Barry was not a rowdy. Quite the opposite. It was noted that the style of his conversation was greatly superior to that usually heard at a mess table in those days. As a matter of fact, there was a certain effeminacy in his manner which he was always striving to overcome.

Please don't get ahead of me. At least before you judge Dr. James Barry too harshly, you'd better learn about the day he passed away.

For this has been the ultimate success story. Yet Dr. Barry was not so much a success for what he did . . . as for what he hid!

James died in London on July 25, 1865. That's when everyone discovered the secret he'd kept for over half a century . . . a secret not even barely suspected by his servant of many years.

When word got out, an official report was immediately sent to the Horse Guards . . . that Dr. James Barry . . . the late Senior Inspector General of the Army Medical Department . . . the highest-ranking medical officer in the United States Army . . . was a woman.

73. THE CAUSE

In June of 1969, Honduras and El Salvador went to war.

Honduras and El Salvador, you'll remember, are two neighboring Central American nations. They're practically cousins.

Honduras is larger than El Salvador; her farmland is better. For years, Salvadorans had gone to Honduras to farm.

No problem. There were the usual suspicions . . . who's in the minority and so on . . . but nothing to fight about—until June of 1969.

That's when Honduras and El Salvador went to war. Why . . . is THE REST OF THE STORY. . . .

It was a matter of national "dishonor," this cause over which the Hondurans decided to fight El Salvador. Their first retaliation was against the Salvadoran farmers living among them.

When the farmers ran home to El Salvador, about fifteen thousand of them, they told of atrocities suffered by them in Honduras.

Some of those atrocities were verified, though most were not. At any rate, both countries broke diplomatic relations and began massive propaganda campaigns.

Within a month, fighting broke out. Five days later, more than two thousand people had been killed, Honduran air attacks had severely damaged El Salvador's industry, and Salvadoran troops were twenty-five miles inside Honduran territory.

Both armies, about five thousand men each, were in disarray. Ammunition and food supplies were unavailable. The air forces, initially about eight planes on each side, were crippled. And the news media had gone bananas. Totally hysterical.

About this time, the OAS stepped in, called for a cease-fire. And they got it . . . for a while.

That was in 1969.

Newspaper headlines read: HONDURAS AND EL SALVADOR, WHERE PEACE REALLY MAY BE AT HAND. It wasn't. It still isn't.

They're *still* going at it down there. Still slugging and sniping away at each other. And back of it all was this mysterious event of national dishonor, supposedly suffered by the Hondurans, the cause over which the two countries separated and have been fighting ever since.

Oh, there are more grievances now, more wind to fan the flame. Doubtless the ingredients for a conflagration always did exist, just waiting for somebody to strike a match.

El Salvador is seriously overpopulated. Her citizens are poor. About 4 million people crowd her 8,260 square miles, giving El Salvador a population density of 485 per square mile. Further complicating this overpopulation problem, El Salvador also has one of the highest birth rates in the world.

Honduras, on the other hand, is underpopulated. Three million people on more than 43,000 square miles. That puts her population density at 70 per square mile, about one seventh that of El Salvador. Yet Honduras is the poorest country in Central America. Its economy, almost entirely agrarian, is growing at a slower rate than that of El Salvador. And although Honduras joined the Central American Common Market with great hopes, it is surely the weakest link in the economy of the region.

So when farmers from overpopulated El Salvador came to underpopulated Honduras to raise crops, things worked out very well. Except for the inevitable jealousy. After all, El Salvador was getting rich off the soil of Honduras!

That was enough to complain about but not enough to fight about.

Until one day in June of 1969. An official of El Salvador made a decision that started a fight, and that fight ignited a war.

Not a government official, an *athletic* official.

What I'm saying is that the eight-year border war that's still going on was triggered by an athletic event. Two Latin American neighbor nations who managed to work together on both sides of an unguarded border for generations are at this moment killing one another over nothing more than a disputed score . . . in a soccer game!

I'll bet you never knew that composer Beethoven visited Louisiana.

If you didn't, don't feel badly.

Neither did Beethoven.

In fact, it was a more circuitous route by which Beethoven's heart and soul reached Dixie . . . a kind of unbroken lineage, you might say. A lineage of pianists and composers.

Consider this: Beethoven's star pupil was a young man named Czerny. Unimpressive-looking, but impressively gifted. Czerny, known as the Father of Scales, practiced them a lot. Perhaps preoccupied himself with them. But he was Beethoven's favorite.

Now, Czerny had a rather famous pupil: Franz Liszt. You know him. He took Czerny's scales and crammed his own compositions full of them . . . lots of romantic flourish from all those dull exercises.

Anyway, among Liszt's brilliant students was Arthur Friedheim, who returned to New York and taught a young girl named O'Bryan . . . Rildia Bee O'Bryan, who went to Shreveport, Louisiana.

And if all this sounds a bit anticlimactic, or if you think the glowing heritage of the great Beethoven dead-ended in a humid, magnolia-laden little hamlet, you'd better know THE REST OF THE STORY.

There's no trick to this Friedheim pupil's name. It's really Rildia Bee O'Bryan and she never so much as entertained the notion of changing it for professional purposes.

No, Rildia Bee O'Bryan was not to change her name until the day she married a petroleum-company landman. Neither was she to become a renowned concert musician, for her parents did not want "that sort of life" for their daughter. Instead, she would become a suburban piano teacher in Shreveport, Louisiana . . . resting at the end of a long, winding road that led back to Beethoven himself.

Or what appeared to be the end.

Eleven years of marriage, no children. Husband Harvey had his petroleum company to attend to and Rildia Bee, her afternoon piano pupils . . . neighborhood school children. But most important of all, Rildia Bee and Harvey had each other. They would not need children of their own to cement their happy marriage.

But as so frequently happens in the lives of those who do not require a special favor, the favor came anyway. After eleven years of marriage, Harvey and Rildia Bee became three.

Harvey had practically to knock over nurses, batter down doors, to see his child born. "No one's going to keep me from being with my wife at a time like this!" And no one did.

It was a boy: Harvey, Jr.

And Rildia Bee never allowed her teaching schedule to conflict with her first obligation as a mother. Lessons were spaced so they would not interfere with baby's nap time. When anything was done, the family would do it together. When anything was to be enjoyed . . . a trip to the movies or a car ride in the country . . . the family would enjoy it together. So it was in an atmosphere of warmth and love and togetherness that young Harvey grew up.

He was, in many ways, a very normal child.

"Mommy," he once said, "I think I'd like to be a taxi driver when I grow up!"

And Mommy smiled.

He saw *Gone with the Wind*, his favorite film, nearly a dozen times before satisfying himself that he'd taken it all in. The drama of it was fascinating to the young boy.

And he had a playhouse in the back yard . . . and neighborhood children to play with . . . and a little girl friend who lived down the street. He was, in very many ways, a very normal child.

But one day, as a mere toddler, he overheard an across-the-fence conversation between his mother and the lady next door.

"No," said the lady, "I don't think we'll ever have children. We've tried, all these years, but now the doctors say it's impossible."

Perhaps she knew that Rildia Bee, herself eleven years childless in marriage, would have a sympathetic word to offer.

But before such a word could be spoken, a tiny voice from behind the back-yard fence chimed in . . .

"Oh, yes!" It was young Harvey, pressing his pudgy face against the wire mesh. "Oh, yes, you'll have *lots* of children! I can see them, right over there!" Pointing to thin air in the neighbor lady's yard, "I can see them . . . they're five little stair steps!"

The lady's eyes grew wide. Quickly, she spun around to see what Harvey was pointing at. There was only a tree . . . and a lawn . . . and nothing more.

The neighbor lady looked down at Harvey, smiling. "That's sweet of you, dear . . . and thank you. But why would I need all those children when I have such a nice little boy right next door?"

"But you'll have them, really you will!" assured Harvey. "I can *see* them!"

And the incident was forgotten. Months passed. Then the lady next door became pregnant. At last, to the amazement of the doctors, she had her child. And another the following year. And another the year after that, until the five "little stair steps" . . . five children in a row . . . materialized out of hopelessness and were playing in the next-door neighbor's back yard, just as Harvey had seen them.

Now, if this was a remarkable coincidence, the coincidences would not stop there. To this day, Harvey's close friends remember the midnight long-distance phone calls. . . .

"I'm sorry to bother you at this hour, but I was lying awake in bed . . . and I got this picture!" He called them "pictures." "You were in the study, sitting on a big upholstered chair I didn't recognize," and the friend would've just come from the study, where he'd been sitting on a newly purchased chair, to answer the phone, "and you were wearing a sort of blue-green shirt," the friend would be wearing a turquoise pull-over, "and you were very sad!"

It never failed. The friend would confess his depression and they'd talk about it, or joke about it, until both felt better and could retire to a good night's sleep.

And Harvey was never truly impressed with this gift of his. After all, it had always been with him. His pleasure was in using it to help others.

If a degree of psychic ability is, as some say, an important facet to even greater talents, then it was true of Harvey.

For there is another chapter in the story of this otherwise very normal youngster. . . .

It was one afternoon, when Harvey was three, that a promising piano pupil had visited their home. Teacher Rildia Bee congratulated her student on a fine rendition of Crawford's *Arpeggio Waltz* . . . told him he'd certainly earned a "gold star" for committing to memory this somewhat advanced piece at the age of only fifteen . . . and adjourned the lesson.

Rildia Bee, later in the kitchen, overheard her pupil back at the keyboard again playing the *Arpeggio Waltz*. She glanced at the clock and went to the kitchen door and called out to the young lad that his mother might be getting anxious . . . that it was time to go home now. . . .

But the music continued, uninterrupted.

Thinking her pupil had not heard, Rildia Bee opened the door to the living room to discover it was not her secondary student at the keyboard. . . .

It was not the considerable accomplishment of a fifteen-year-old boy she was rehearsing. There at the piano, having had no lesson in his life, but playing by ear . . . was three-year-old Harvey.

I'd guess the tears that welled into the teacher's eyes that afternoon were mixed with pride and reservation. None knew better than she what a monumental career might await a pianist so accomplished at three, and yet what dedication and discipline and inevitable sacrifice it would require.

There was no turning back now. There was a pianist in the family. And under her guidance that boy grew to match, then surpass, the artistry of his gifted mother.

The days became years, the minuet became Rachmaninoff . . . the pudgy little boy grew lean and tall at the keyboard. After a bout with typhoid, the board-straight hair grew thick and curly. Soon, the tiny hands became huge, powerful, sensitive.

And one day, when he was ready, there was an international competition in Moscow . . . and Harvey would win hands down.

You know the rest, or at least you should . . . that the winding path from Beethoven to the Bayous would not end there.

And though Harvey was a young lad of two distinct gifts, the world remembers one.

He was christened Harvey Lavan Cliburn, Jr.

But since the day he was born, his parents called him . . . Van.

Dear Abby,

I never thought I would be writing to you.

Here all these years you have been advising others, coun-
seling others, cheering up the rest of us.

Now apparently it's you who need cheering up.

All right . . . *I'll* try to help you with *your* problem.

That letter from you, dated November 22, sounded
dreadful. What have you ever done that was worthwhile,
you ask. Indeed!

If you'll pardon my saying so you sound like one of those
people always writing to you for encouragement when
their problems are so comparatively trivial that they don't
even deserve to be reprinted.

But I know how it is. Sometimes we get so close to our
own personal problems that it takes an outsider to help us
see over the top of them.

And that is what motivated this letter from me to you.

What have you done that you can look back upon with

pride and pleasure? My goodness, Abby, I won't even mention your admiring and your adoring public.

How about your family? For anything which went wrong there you certainly cannot blame yourself.

I remember those years when your lawyer husband was away so much . . . when you had to bring up the youngsters almost alone. And yet you continued your writing.

Isn't that accomplishment a source of pride and pleasure?

We who have admired the way you reply to the letters of others . . . always with such good sense, always so encouraging . . . how ironic that one of us now should be seeking to console *you*.

But your November 22 letter reflects on what you call "your many follies and errors of judgment."

Surely, dear Abby, you who have been so understanding of others are now being much too rough on yourself.

Why, I remember reading about your experiences in London when you encountered considerable discourtesy and yet responded with such grace; I remember thinking that Abby is capable of rising above any circumstance.

We read with envy about your adventures in Paris and in Washington, hobnobbing with all those important people.

Abby, you are so admired by everyone, just everyone! That is why it is so difficult for an admirer to realize that you are really serious in that last letter when you wrote, "What have I done . . . that I can look back upon with pleasure?"

Abby, I hesitate to mention this. But didn't you have a birthday recently? November eleven, wasn't it?

That'll do it sometimes.

Birthdays and the sometimes housewifely frustration of facing the same chores for as far ahead as you can see.

However liberated women are becoming—and certainly you more than most—it will be a long time if ever before women really catch up. The more capable a woman is the more she resents that.

Also it occurs to me that you, being the daughter of a clergyman, might tend to demand too much of yourself.

Abby, I'm afraid I've not succeeded very well in what I set out to do, to encourage you.

But try to believe me that anybody looking at your exciting and fruitful life . . . and then reading that last letter from you (I have a copy of it in front of me in your handwriting) . . . I mean, my dear Abby, to sum up such a lifetime as yours and to ask, as you do, the forgiveness of God for not having accomplished more?

Shame on you! Shame on you, Abigail Smith Adams! Do you count it as "nothing" that you were the wife of a President of the United States? And the mother of another one!

No other woman in American history can make that statement.

Love,
P A

76. THE LAUNCHING OF THE LITTLE RED WAGON

I'm about to tell you about a little boy who saw things differently.

Toys weren't toys . . . they were transportation.

Firecrackers weren't firecrackers . . . they were energy.

The fact that he saw life differently eventually changed the shape of the modern world.

We can trace his influence on us to the turning point in his life . . . when he was thirteen years old. But that's THE REST OF THE STORY.

The little boy who saw things differently was born to wealthy parents who hoped for a distinguished career for their son. Perhaps that's why Dad was so disturbed at his son's interest in dangerous explosives. What would the boy be when he grew up . . . a safe-cracker?

The young lad protested that his "dangerous explosives" were actually no more than firecrackers and skyrockets. They were mar-velous sources of energy . . . sources of power that could be tapped constructively. To his Dad, however, they were dangerous.

The boy was thirteen. He'd obtained some skyrockets from a friend, six of them, and he sat alone on the porch steps one after-noon, trying to figure out how they might best be put to use.

Idly, he looked out over the front lawn . . . and over to his lit-tle red wagon . . . and then it hit him. If just *one* of those skyrockets could lift itself high into the sky, then maybe . . . just maybe *six* of them could take his *wagon* into the stratosphere!

The lad slipped back into the house . . . "Mom? Dad?" he called. No one answered. Good. Yet they might return at any moment, so he'd have to act fast.

Quickly he looked about for some rope or sturdy twine or anything that would secure the rockets to his wagon. When he found it, he tied two rockets to either side . . . and the remaining two in the back . . . and then, with his heart pounding in anticipation of the little red wagon's solo flight . . . he lit the fuses.

The lad jumped clear, fully expecting his contraption to take off straight up. Then came the big surprise. The blast of the first skyrocket to ignite tipped the wagon over . . . back on its wheels! By the time the rest of the skyrockets had ignited, the little red wagon project had aborted . . . and the little red wagon itself was careening down the street at an amazing speed!

When the boy saw this, he was at first stunned . . . and perhaps a bit disappointed . . . but at last he was overcome with joy. The rockets were powering his wagon . . . it *was* moving because of them, faster than he could ever pull it. With an elated burst of enthusiasm, the boy bolted down the street after the little red wagon.

When the skyrockets finally burned out, five blocks down, it was with a magnificent explosion. Neighbors ran from their houses to see what had happened, and there they saw a breathless, exuberant young boy, dancing about the charred chassis of a childhood toy.

And then the police arrived.

What was going on here? they demanded to know.

It worked, it worked! was all the lad could say. And the ecstatic youngster was quickly taken into custody.

When Dad arrived to bail his son out, the boy was still excited over his conquest. Although the child was reprimanded severely, he never got over the excitement.

But Dad eventually overcame his own fear of an undistinguished career for his boy. For the lad grew to distinguish himself as no other ever has in the field of rocketry technology.

The boy whose toys ceased to be toys went on to achieve his

doctorate at twenty-two. So respected was he that his country called on him to head its rocket research.

But his country wasn't ours. Not at first, anyway. There was a long patch of sky between the red wagon and the Redstone. At the age of twenty-four, the young man whose very first experiment got him arrested, was making rockets . . . for Hitler.

You've heard of Peenemunde. . . where he worked.

You know the V-2 . . . that lashed London.

But when the Allies were closing in . . . and surrender was between the Russians and the Americans . . . he accepted the country that accepted God . . . and came to work for us.

Without him, we could never have answered the Sputnik.

Without him, there would be no Saturn V . . . the Saturn V that carried men to the moon.

And all because a little boy in a German suburb thought he could make his wagon fly.

In a way, it did not.

And in a way, it reached the stars.

As you know well by now, his name was Wernher von Braun . . . and now you also know THE REST OF THE STORY.

Gladys was a beautiful woman with a taste for Norwegian men.
Edward was a tall, handsome Norwegian with a taste for fast motorcycles.

Back in the twenties, Gladys and Edward were lovers . . . and
they had a child.

Edward Mortenson had been born in Norway in 1897. He
started out as a baker's apprentice, later opened his own bakery.

Ed eventually got married, had three children, developed a lust
for fast motorcycles and fast women, deserted his family in 1923,
came to the United States.

He became an itinerant baker, working briefly in one city and
then traveling on to another. He left in his wake a trail of pie
crusts and pastry icing . . . and broken hearts.

Gladys was just one of those broken hearts.

Gladys' earlier husband had deserted her. She was alone and
had few friends, when along came Ed, the Don Juan doughboy
from Norway.

Things went well between Gladys and Ed for a while.

Gladys knew about Ed's past. But this time it seemed as though
Ed might settle down. She couldn't have known that it always
seemed that way.

One day, Gladys told Ed that she was pregnant. Ed just looked at her . . . expressionless . . . said nothing.

They might get married, suggested Gladys. They might get married and give their child a good home. After all, Ed had a job and with their combined salaries. . . .

Still Ed said nothing. He turned . . . went out the door . . . got on his motorcycle.

Gladys never saw him again.

For many months, Ed stayed on the road, traveling from town to town. He took a job baking one place . . . took a lover the next . . . the eternal cookie Casanova.

The girls went for his Norwegian accent and he went for the girls. But he always got back on his motorcycle. An uneasy rider with a child somewhere whom he would never meet.

Yet this one rejected responsibility began to haunt him. What would it grow up to be . . . a bum, like himself? An endless searcher with a string of broken hearts?

Ed would never know the answer. On June 18 of 1929, on a road leading from Youngstown to Akron, Ohio, Ed tried to pass a car on his motorcycle. He met head on with a Hudson sedan. He fell to the ground, unconscious, both legs broken, paralyzed. His motorcycle was in pieces.

In a few hours, at the hospital, Ed died.

He was buried in a pauper's grave in Youngstown . . . virtually forgotten though the father of one of Hollywood's most publicized stars. That is THE REST OF THE STORY.

Although Ed was gone, the trail of broken hearts would lead on and on.

Ed's little girl . . . his daughter by Gladys . . . would walk it alone . . . through the heat of camera lights and the cold of white chiffon.

She became: Marilyn Monroe.

78. THE OLD MAN AND THE GULLS

About sunset it happened every Friday evening, on a lonely stretch along the eastern Florida seacoast. You could see an old man walking, white-haired, bushy-eyebrowed, slightly bent.

One gnarled hand would be gripping the handle of a pail, a large bucket filled with shrimp. There, on a broken pier reddened by the setting sun, the weekly ritual would be re-enacted.

At once, the silent twilight sky would become a mass of dancing dots . . . growing larger. In the distance, screeching calls would become louder.

They were sea gulls, come from nowhere, on the same pilgrimage . . . to meet an old man.

For half an hour or so, the gentleman would stand on the pier, surrounded by fluttering white, till his pail of shrimp was empty.

But the gulls would linger for a while. Perhaps one would perch comfortably on the old man's hat . . . and a certain day gone by would gently come to mind.

Eventually, all of the old man's days were past. If the gulls still return to that spot . . . perhaps on a Friday evening at sunset . . . it is not for food . . . but to pay homage to the secret they shared with a gentle stranger.

And that secret is THE REST OF THE STORY.

Anyone who remembers October of 1942 remembers the day it was reported that Captain Eddie Rickenbacker was lost at sea.

Captain Eddie's mission had been to deliver a message of the utmost importance to General MacArthur. MacArthur was head-quartered in New Guinea, and Rickenbacker was given a B-17 and a hand-picked crew to take him there.

But there was an unexpected detour which would hurl Captain Eddie into the most harrowing adventure of his life.

Somewhere over the South Pacific the Flying Fortress became lost beyond the reach of radio. Fuel ran dangerously low, so the men ditched their plane in the ocean.

The B-17 stayed afloat just long enough for all aboard to get out. Then, slowly, the tail of the Flying Fortress swung up and poised for a split second . . . and the ship went down, leaving eight men and three rafts . . . and the horizon.

For nearly a month Captain Eddie and his companions would fight the water, and the weather, and the scorching sun.

They spent many sleepless nights recoiling as giant sharks rammed their rafts. The largest raft was nine by five. The biggest shark . . . ten feet long.

But of all their enemies at sea, one proved most formidable: starvation. Eight days out, their rations were long gone or de-stroyed by the salt water. It would take a miracle to sustain them. And a miracle occurred.

In Captain Eddie's own words, "Cherry," that was the B-17 pilot, Captain William Cherry, "read the service that afternoon, and we finished with a prayer for deliverance and a hymn of praise. There was some talk, but it tapered off in the oppressive heat. With my hat pulled down over my eyes to keep out some of the glare, I dozed off."

Now this is still Captain Rickenbacker talking . . . "Something landed on my head. I knew that it was a sea gull. I don't know how I knew, I just knew.

"Everyone else knew too. No one said a word, but peering out from under my hat brim without moving my head, I could see the expression on their faces. They were staring at that gull. The gull meant food . . . if I could catch it."

And the rest, as they say, is history.

Captain Eddie caught the gull. Its flesh was eaten. Its intestines were used for bait to catch fish. The survivors were sustained and their hopes renewed because a lone sea gull, uncharacteristically hundreds of miles from land, offered itself as a sacrifice.

You know that Captain Eddie made it.

And now you also know . . . that he never forgot.

Because every Friday evening, about sunset . . . on a lonely stretch along the eastern Florida seacoast . . . you could see an old man walking . . . white-haired, bushy-eyebrowed, slightly bent.

His bucket filled with shrimp was to feed the gulls . . . to remember that one which, on a day long past, gave itself without a struggle . . . like manna in the wilderness.

79. DARK CHRISTMAS

Christmas Night. 1776.

A silent, swift race with the devil . . . a race against time.

In the darkness, a quiet panic gripped General Washington's men. And as the black air grew colder, the tension among them increased.

Conditions for the crossing had worsened throughout the night. The Delaware was high and flowing fast. Gigantic blocks of ice were in the river now, and new ice had begun to form. Unless this sinister water could be negotiated, their planned attack on Trenton would fail.

A powerful wind was whipping over the Delaware . . . driving, relentless. As it lashed at the long, light-draft boats, even the trained seamen of Glover's Regiment began to wonder if Fate were entirely against them.

Deadline for the crossing had been midnight, now long since passed. The loading of eighteen field cannons on the narrow boats was painfully slow work. The organization of troops and the treachery of the river had pressed them into the early morning. The morning after Christmas. It was 3 A.M. before the mission was accomplished; the ice was behind them. Our artillery was unloaded on New Jersey soil.

By 4:00 A.M., General Washington's men were deployed. In

three hours, it would be light. There were nine miles of road to cover, two and a half thousand troops to move. And the enemy was sleeping . . . at Trenton.

You know what happened at Trenton, two hundred Christmases ago. First contact with the enemy at 8 A.M. . . . final surrender before ten o'clock. Not one American life had been lost. And it would never have come to pass had General George Washington not bet against the odds . . . had the dark Delaware not been crossed that Christmas Night.

The scene has been immortalized in a painting, and though you're certainly familiar with it, I don't think you know THE REST OF THE STORY.

Of all the stirring patriotic portraits, perhaps none is so popular . . . so well known world-wide . . . as "Washington Crossing the Delaware." You know the one: General George standing in the bow of a Durham boat, facing an ice-ravaged river . . . crew members laboring at the oars, some prodding the ice away . . . flag rippling in the wind . . . one can practically feel the stinging sleet by merely observing it.

Now, I know it's the fashion to pick apart great works of art . . . to detect some small indiscretion, something that could not possibly have been. But we're not going to do that here. Because there's something even more remarkable about the painting.

In the first place, there were actually three paintings of "Washington Crossing the Delaware" . . . same artist, three separate versions. One suffered damage in a fire, was subsequently lost. Another was moved in 1851 to the Metropolitan Museum of Art in New York City. An impressive work, it hangs there still. But the third version . . . the one you know . . . hung in the White House until September of 1973. At that time it was put up for auction and was purchased privately the following year for $260,000. The current owner, one Duane Hillmer of Omaha, Nebraska, released that precious painting during the bicentennial year to the Düsseldorf Art Museum in Germany.

In Germany? That's right . . . the painting had gone home!

This All-American masterwork was painted seventy-five years after the event . . . and it was painted by a German artist in Germany!

And one wonders if he knew then what the admirers of this borrowed exhibit do not seem to know now.

That our George was not crossing the river that night to fight the British . . . but to fight Germans.

80. BELL'S BELLES

Once upon a time there was a speech therapist . . . a school-teacher speech therapist whose compassion for deaf children was so great that he drew up plans for an invention. This invention, said the therapist, would "hear" for the deaf . . . would render sound waves visible, identifiable, to those who could not perceive them otherwise. If the therapist's machine was a success, his little deaf students would be able to see speech as others hear it.

The machine was a failure. Almost.

Because, in the process of time, that unsuccessful apparatus became the telephone of today. The speech therapist . . . the schoolteacher who started out working with deaf children . . . was Alexander Graham Bell.

But you just *think* you know THE REST OF THE STORY. . . .

Now, if it's true that behind every great man is a woman, then it was doubly true of Alexander. There were two women in Aleck's life . . . two ladies who greatly inspired him: his mother and his wife.

Bell's mother, Eliza, was a teacher. She directed his childhood attention to acoustics and particularly to the study of speech. Whenever Aleck set about on his various youthful enterprises and hobbies, Eliza was always there to encourage him. But she never interfered. She never got in his way. She knew that Aleck would have to find out certain things for himself. And he did.

It wasn't long before Aleck and his brother had invented a machine that could talk. It had lungs and vocal cords and a mouth and a tongue. And what were its first words? "Mama," of course.

Yes, there can be no doubt that the original "Ma Bell" was a marvelous inspiration to young Aleck. In fact, so concerned were Bell's parents that Aleck speak English without an accent, that when the young man finally came to teach school in Boston, no one could tell he had been born in Scotland.

Enter Mabel Hubbard . . . the second belle in Bell's life . . . his future wife.

Mabel's daddy was one of Aleck's earliest acquaintances in Boston. She, the beautiful young daughter, had recently returned from school in Germany. From there on, the story of Alexander Graham Bell and Mabel Hubbard weaves the romantic tapestry of a nineteenth-century novel.

She, youthful, lovely, rich.

He, brilliant, ardent, poor.

Together they would encounter the traditionally romantic obstacles of parental objection, despair, ridicule of his genius. And yes, they eventually succeeded. Fame and fortune became theirs. And yes, they lived happily ever after. Mabel's daddy even became first director of the Bell Telephone Company, in 1877.

Of Bell and his wife it was once said: Their story is as thoroughly unspoiled and charming as a story can be.

It was true. Mabel, like Aleck's mother, Eliza, inspired Bell through love and through devotion to him . . . and perhaps, in many ways, through something else.

Alexander Bell's primary interest was speech and speech therapy. His occupation, first and foremost, was his work with those who could not hear. Isn't it ironic, then, that his beloved students could never benefit from his most celebrated invention, the telephone?

Yes, and it is even more ironic when you consider that Bell's belles . . . his mother and his wife . . . the two women who inspired him the most . . . could never fully appreciate it either.

For they also . . . his mother and his wife . . . they, too . . . were deaf.

81. WINCHESTER CATHEDRAL

This is the kind of story that ought to be saved for a campfire or for a cold, rainy night. Remember that when you pass it along.

Sarah was an heiress. A woman with money. Lots of it. And she was alone.

She had little family, to begin with. Her only child, Annie, died at five weeks. Then her husband passed away, and Sarah, the society belle of New Haven, Connecticut, was without anyone.

The year was 1884, Sarah had her twenty-million-dollar inheritance and her additional income of one thousand dollars a day, but for a woman of forty-seven . . . a woman childless . . . a woman with only memories of love . . . the money seemed little comfort indeed.

Sixteen years before the turn of the century, Sarah left New Haven and moved across the continent to San Jose, California. She bought an eight-room farmhouse from a doctor named Caldwell. It was there that Sarah would live alone until she died. What happened during those mysterious thirty-eight years is THE REST OF THE STORY.

Immediately after purchasing her farmhouse, Sarah bought a hundred and sixty surrounding acres. Then she called in a team of sixteen carpenters and started to work. A remodeling project was

under way that would keep craftsmen working around the clock
. . . every day, including holidays . . . for thirty-eight years.

It became obvious to the workmen from the very beginning
that this project was more than the whim of an eccentric heiress.
There was an eerie tinge to each of her instructions. For instance,
each window must have thirteen panes, each wall thirteen panels,
each closet thirteen hooks, each chandelier thirteen globes.

There were plans for miles of winding corridors, some leading
nowhere. One door would open on a blank wall, another on a
fifty-foot drop. One set of stairs would lead into a closed ceiling.
Peculiar and chilling designs like the spider web and the pen-
tagram were everywhere.

There would be rooms riddled with trap doors and an infinity
of secret passageways and one particular blue room . . . to be entered only by the widow Sarah.

It was obvious from the very beginning that this was to be more
than an estate of oddities for a restless recluse. It was to be an oc-
cult cathedral. A home for the dead.

In a short while, a bell tower was erected. Every night at midnight, a trusted servant would descend into an underground laby-
rinth and make the only passageway connection to the tower.
Then he'd ring the solitary bell . . . to call in the spirits . . . and
Sarah would enter the blue room. At 2:00 A.M., the servant would
ring the bell again, bidding the ghosts to return to their graves.
On and on, every night . . . for thirty-eight years.

Construction of this poltergeist palace did not end until at last
Sarah died, at eighty-five. By that time, the house had spread over
six acres of the estate, had a hundred and sixty rooms, ten thousand windows, four hundred and sixty-seven doors, fifty-two sky-
lights, forty-seven fireplaces, forty stairways, thirteen bathrooms,
and six kitchens.

While Sarah was alive, her carpenters and servants never saw
their mistress as anything but a slight, veiled figure not even five
feet tall. She must have seemed a ghost herself, flitting about the
monstrous, peopleless mansion. Sarah lived her life for the dead
. . . and one moonlit night, she joined them.

If you're ever in San Jose, you can take a tour of that house . . .
but only by day. For tour guides don't venture into the mansion
at night. Frightening noises, they say. And caretakers confirm

there are still sounds of heavy breathing . . . still footsteps in the otherwise midnight silence.

If it's true, they belong to the widow Sarah Winchester and the legion of phantoms she befriended . . . out of guilt.

You see, her inheritance came from the Winchester rifle . . . the weapon that killed more Indians and more U.S. soldiers than any other in our nation's early history.

Sarah built her mansion . . . so *they* would have a home.

EPILOGUE: THEN THERE WERE THREE

No one remembers the exact date THE REST OF THE STORY was conceived.

What we know for certain is that the form of THE REST OF THE STORY began with Paul Harvey, and he has been using it in publications and on radio and on television for more than a quarter of a century.

THE REST OF THE STORY is actually his way of looking at history and lives. It doesn't exist outside the point of view of the telling. But so popular has Mr. Harvey's formula become that the phrase THE REST OF THE STORY has been adopted into everyday usage. The concealed fact or figure . . . the sense of living before the event . . . that's THE REST OF THE STORY.

Until recently, there's been only one person who wrote for Paul Harvey: his wife. But the task of being Paul Harvey's editor, manager, and producer is quite enough for anyone. Even for Angel.

So the past two decades have been spent in a sort of manhunt, a search for someone who could re-create the Harvey style of writing. The difficulty of this search has resulted in Mr. Harvey's getting up very early each morning and pounding every word of his broadcasts, columns, speeches, and stories into a typewriter one at a time . . . by himself.

That's where I come in . . . I'm Paul Aurandt.

I've been a musician most of my life. A concert pianist. I've written a fair amount of music, too. But the writing of words . . . well, it seemed like magic to me.

I've always been a fan of Paul Harvey. The quality of his voice and the timing of his words never failed to mesmerize me, even as a young boy who understood little of the News. I listened to him every day, at the encouragement of my parents. And I suppose you might say that the Paul Harvey timing even influenced my music later. The dramatic pauses, the careful, warm pacing.

Anyway, I had known for quite some while that Paul Harvey, my childhood hero, was looking for a writer. On an impulse one day . . . when I was practicing for an upcoming concert . . . I sat down and wrote a REST OF THE STORY just as I imagined Paul Harvey would have written it. The topic was a musical one . . . something I'd researched once.

When I was finished, I showed the story to my mother . . . another Paul Harvey devotee. And she was impressed! "It sounds just like him!" she told me.

To make a long story short, I applied for and got the job. I've had to set aside a lot of concerts, but I'm really having fun. So far, at least.

Oh, there's something you might be interested in learning about Mr. Harvey. When you work for someone, you learn things about him no one else knows.

Paul Harvey is not his complete name.

Now, don't tell anybody you heard it from me, but Harvey is his middle name. He dropped his last name because it was difficult to spell and to pronounce.

I kept it.

I'm his son.

And now you know the rest . . . of THE REST OF THE STORY.